JANUSZ KORCZAK

GHETTO DIARY

JANUSZ KORCZAK

GHETTO DIARY

Aaron Zeitlin
The Last Walk
of Janusz Korczak

HOLOCAUST LIBRARY
New York

JANUSZ KORCZAK:
GHETTO DIARY

Janusz Korczak: Ghetto Diary
Copyright © 1978 by Holocaust Library
Aaron Zeitlin: The Last Walk of Janusz Korczak
Copyright © 1978 by Rachel Zeitlin

Library of Congress Catalog Card Number: 77-91911
Publication of this book was made possible by a
grant from Benjamin and Stefa Wald

Jacket design by Eric Gluckman
Printed in the United States of America

CONTENTS

Page

The Last Walk of Janusz Korczak
by Aaron Zeitlin 7

GHETTO DIARY
by Janusz Korczak

Preface by Igor Newerly 67

Part One 77

Part Two 153

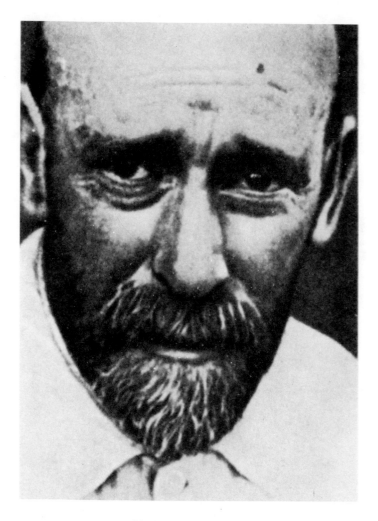

JANUSZ KORCZAK

THE LAST WALK OF JANUSZ KORCZAK

A Prose Poem

1. THE KARL MARX OF THE CHILDREN

There is a city; its body still exists but its soul is gone. For the Jews were its soul.

In a poverty-stricken neighborhood of that city, on Krochmalna Street, a healer of the sick had built up his dream: a three-story building in which he planned to establish the world's first children's republic.

In the attic of that three-story building on 92 Krochmalna Street there often sat a baldheaded man, neither tall nor short, with eyeglasses and a yellowish goatee. Sometimes he wore a shabby uniform dating back to his days as an army doctor; on other occasions, he had on a green surgical apron, which he had not had the chance—or perhaps the desire—to take off. His reason for still wearing his old uniform from time to time probably was to poke fun at those who stood in awe of uniforms—or perhaps it was a gesture of protest against those who had the effrontery to link the art of healing with the bloodshed of war.

He had served as an army doctor for a long time, first during the war between Russia and Japan, then during the first world slaughter of 1914–18, and finally during the civil war in Russia, where he had wandered about, homeless, until he had been able to return to Poland. As for the green surgical apron, he liked it because of its color; green was the symbol of hope, of youth, of new beginnings. He still remembered from his student days

7

in Berlin what Goethe had said in *Faust*: "Green is the golden tree of life." Oh, he knew very well that life was far from golden; besides, social visionary that he was, gold meant nothing to him except when it appeared in a sunset. But he hoped that the day would come when everything would be different and when he would be the one who had helped hasten the change.

Ironically, there was gold even in his name. He had been born Hersh Goldszmit. But he had considered Polish, not Yiddish, as his mother tongue, and so he had taken a Polish given name—Henryk. In time, however, he had become known not only in Poland but in many other lands, too, as Janusz Korczak. This had been the pen name (he had begun to write at the age of 14) with which he had signed his essays, and later also his books. As the years passed, Janusz Korczak became his name even more than the one he had been given at birth.

During his student days, he had made a short trip to Switzerland. There, he had met a Jewish girl from Warsaw, who had been studying in Switzerland and Belgium. Her name was Stefania Wilczynska. She was tall and self-assured, and she had a mischievous sparkle in her dark eyes. The daughter of a wealthy family, she was beholden to no one and defiantly waited for someone who would be able to make her do his bidding. She was younger and taller than Korczak, but the mischievous little flames that danced in her eyes began to flicker in humble wonderment as if swept by a gust of wind, when Korczak, sitting beside her on a park bench one day, said to her: "You know, I am the son of a madman," and, with a grimace that had been intended as, but in fact was not, a smile, he added that he had resolved, at the very first opportunity, to become the "Karl Marx of the children."

She listened quietly to his monologue, interrupting him only with a word now and then.

He told her that he had come from a wealthy, assimilated family which had come to grief after his father, a well-known lawyer, had become insane and had had to be placed into a mental hospital. As a result, the full burden of supporting the family had fallen upon him, the oldest of the children. Still almost a child himself, he had learned early what it meant to have to turn to grownups for help. Even more than before his father's illness, when his father insulted him and called him a stupid ass, the boy had felt the insensitivity and cruelty with which the grown-up world treated its children and its young people. He had never forgotten the cold, idiotic contempt with which one Polish writer, the editor of a well-known magazine, had flung back into his face one of his first rapturous attempts at poetry. As might have been expected of a youth his age, it had been a love poem; in it, he had written that he was ready to die of despair. And the great editor had asked him, "So what's keeping you?"

"And do you know," said the young student to the girl on the park bench, speaking more to himself than to her, "why this man had the effrontery to speak to me like that? Simply because he was a person of privilege. Not just because he was an editor and a famous writer, too, but because he felt that he was speaking to a mere boy." Adulthood in itself is a privilege, and therefore the first step in any struggle against privilege would have to be the eradication of this false privilege of adulthood.

"That sounds interesting," the young girl said. "Tell me more about your father."

For answer, the young man launched into another monologue. He recalled that whenever he had visited his father in his hospital cell, the sick man would say to him over and over again: "Man is forever under siege . . . and who will lift that siege? No one, no one ever."

9

For years, it turned out, his father had been hounded by creatures whom he had named "the mockers." Their mockery had been so grotesque that it had made even their victim laugh. He had discovered that these creatures hated it when a mere human returned their laughter. Whenever he started to poke fun at them, they would disappear. They would return again and again, but it did them no good. However, there were others who had made his father truly miserable: these he called the tormentors. "You will never be able to destroy their kind with laughter," his father had told him. The sick man's first encounter with one of them had been in the courtroom. He had been defending a prisoner whose innocence had been so obvious that he would never have been found guilty, had it not been for the man-like demon whose shadow had appeared behind the judges. The mockers wanted to make others feel small, to show them their nothingness, their inability even to understand that there was something amiss with them. They were the wags, the magicians, the acrobats of a mysterious circus, and their god was a pinhead. But a man's real enemies were the tormentors. They found their servants and minions among living men. Injustice, misfortune, bloodshed—all this was their work. When their servants, the living people, died, these, too, turned into demons, and as long as this would continue, there could be no justice in the world. They were the ones who dictated the law and, as any freshman at law school can tell you, law and justice are not the same thing. The sick man had seen more than his share of tormentors in the courtroom. "Man, the human species, is forever under siege," he had told his son.

"There they are!" the father had cried out. "There they are, the tormentors! Can't you see them, fool?"

The father had cowered in a corner, hidden his ashen

10

face in his hands and trembled. Then he had leaped to his feet, grabbed his son by the shoulders, shaken him and thrown him out of the room.

Now, as he told the story, the student cast sidelong glances at Stefania from time to time. He could sense every tremor that passed through her body.

"Do you know," he said to her, almost solemnly, "I felt that there was some truth in my father's insane imaginings."

"Some truth?"

"Yes," he replied, with a half-sad, half-mischievous look. "Man is forever under siege from powers that are not human. Sometimes the mockers visit me, too. After all, I am my father's son. And how do I deal with them? I do exactly what my father did. The prescription is simple: laugh back into their faces. As for the tormentors, I have not yet had the pleasure of meeting any of them—I mean those tormentors whom my father saw behind the backs of the judges and the police. But I have the honor to inform you that I have inherited from my father other symptoms of abnormality, which he showed even when he was still normal. However, abnormality does not remain the same forever. It is, in fact, sub-normality and can be transformed into super-normality. My ambition is to become super-normal."

"A genius, then?" Stefania asked.

"I don't know. Let us not use such words lightly. As far as I know myself, I am blessed with a paradoxical sense of humor. But at the same time I have inherited from my father a melancholy streak. In me, that streak brings forth flashes of lightning. But if I should ever marry and have children, they would inherit only the streak and would only add to the misery already in this world."

Stefania Wilczynska gave him a long, curious look.

"What do you intend to do, then?" she asked, not

realizing that she was addressing him with the intimate *ty* instead of the formal *pan*.

"What I intend to do? I will fight against those who attack men and against those who do the bidding of these creatures. I am my father's son, but I am not a weakling. I will not surrender. I will not hide in a corner and tremble. Let the enemies be afraid of man, and not man afraid of them. We must work with the children. We must see to it that the children should break the siege ring within which man has been confined. To begin with, children must have the right to govern themselves—the right of absolute self-government."

Stefania smiled. "Why, even the grownups can't help themselves, and yet you expect that children. . . ."

"Yes. That is what I want."

"But that's absurd."

He laughed. "I have already told you that I am my father's son and that I also have some abnormalities of my own. For instance, one day there was a students' meeting. I listened to the speeches and kept quiet. Then, all of a sudden, I got up from my seat and asked for permission to speak. And what did I say? Nothing, really. Only one sentence: 'I hereby wish to inform my colleagues that they and all the other careerists can go to hell.' That was all. With that, I left the hall, whistling a tune. . . . All this happened quite suddenly . . . No one had expected it and, frankly, neither had I."

The little specks in Stefania's eyes began to flicker merrily. "But that was just a game."

"But I didn't just say that they could go to hell; I said something that cannot be repeated to a lady."

"Anti-bourgeoisie?"

"I went off to the proletarians and tutored their children without pay. May Day, the 'Red Banner,' the Revolution! I still like the 'Red Banner,' but red is not my color. Proletarian misery, indeed! What are the proletarians after? The affluence of the rich.

"I wandered through the dark streets of the Old City of Warsaw. I sought out the worst of the misery, the corners where the prostitutes were standing by the streetlights. I myself felt like an ancient whore dragging along some ancient drunkard, against his will, because not even he wanted any business with her. I wanted to become a prophet of their kind of misery, which I saw as the misery of all mankind. At night, in a tavern in the Old City, I saw a man beating another until he drew blood. The mob inside was enjoying the spectacle. I rushed up to the two and kissed the aggressor on his vicious, pockmarked face. I begged him to stop beating the other man. Taken aback by my kiss, the man stopped for a moment. There was thunderous laughter. They were all laughing: the knife pullers, the lushes, the pimps and the whores—everybody."

"And the man who got the beating?"

"He was laughing at me also. And at that moment I saw it all in a flash which refused to vanish. Their laughter recalled to me how the grownups had laughed at me when I was a child, whenever I said something that children know but grownups do not understand. Misery? Proletariat? The world's oldest proletariat is the *child*. This, the oldest underdog in the world, is suffering at the hands of those who call themselves grownups. The child is hounded even by those who love him. Kisses, too, can kill. We must make a start with the oldest underdog in the world—the child. Justice will come forth from the Children's International."

"Why talk about children?" Stefania retorted with a touch of annoyance. "Only a few minutes ago you said you did not want any children."

13

"I do want to have children, but not just two, or three. I want hundreds of them! Hundreds!"

"Indeed?"

The student's eyes took on a far-away look.

"I will finish my studies in pediatrics. I will work at children's hospitals, and then I will build up a model institution. I will be a father of orphans. . . ."

"Why a father of orphans? It seems to me that this would be a privilege reserved for God. At least that is what the clergy would have us believe."

"A child is an orphan even if he has two living parents. How much more an orphan, then, is a child who does not even have a roof over his head! Children should come first, but they are always put last. I will build up a children's society for my orphans, and out of that society the Children's Republic will grow. These children will not be tortured. No! Not they!"

"A Children's Republic?" Stefania repeated as if repeating a verse from a poem.

"They will govern themselves; they will have their own courts of justice and a parliament. And in time there will be a Children's International."

"Karl Marx Goldszmit!" Stefania attempted to turn it into a joke. But she felt herself falling in love with him, and so she touched his hand and said:

"It's a beautiful, crazy idea, just like one of Juliusz Slowacki's poems . . ."[1]

She had always loved Slowacki's poetry.

2. THE ORPHANS' REPUBLIC

The doctor at the Children's Hospital on Sliska Street

---

1. Juliusz Slowacki (1809–49), Polish romantic-messianic poet.

14

insists on wearing a shabby coat, even though he has more money than he needs to live on and there is no lack of doctors who envy him. With his shiny pants and seedy-looking eyeglasses over his myopic eyes, eyes which look dusty as if ashamed of their blueness, he looks like an unkempt elderly student who earns pennies as a tutor and has a hard time making ends meet. But in fact this children's doctor has become famous. He turns out books with ease, one after the other. He enjoys dropping a rude remark now and then, and pokes fun at the dressed-up ladies and elegant gentlemen. He snaps his fingers at high society, even though the Polish aristocrats trust him sufficiently to have him treat their sick children and have given him a good reputation. But to him all this is no more than a start toward the fulfillment of his own dreams: the orphans' home. Stefa can hardly wait, because *her* dream is to live under one roof with Korczak, no matter what people will say.

And now at last the house is ready, a big three-story building complete with a basement. Stefa Wilczynska is the housemother. The children call her Miss Stefa. A long time ago she left Western Europe and returned to Warsaw. She has left the home of her wealthy parents and is spending her days and nights on Krochmalna Street.

In the attic of the three-story building there is a little room where the doctor goes to rest whenever he is tired or troubled. Sometimes he catches himself praying, though he does not know to whom. These are prayers without words. *"Prayers of an Unbeliever,"* he calls them. Sometimes the mockers—his inheritance from his father—turn up in the middle of the day to insult him, and then he retreats with them to his attic chamber and stays there until they leave him. At such times a wall can turn into a long, thin stick-file on which one prescription

15

blank has been skewered. A hand appears, pushes the prescription blank back and covers it with other prescriptions. There is no way of knowing whether they are thoughts or living things. They assort themselves, form a line, but remain skewered one atop the other. they bellow at one another and push each other, falling to the ground with an uproar, but then the hand reaches down and spears them onto a stick-file again. They hang one atop the other on the stick-file like so many slaughtered geese on a meathook. Wags join hands, bowing like actors at the end of their performance. Then they stretch out like rulers, and put out their tongues at the doctor. A long face, rising like a storm-ravaged tree in an El Greco painting, grows longer and narrower until it becomes like a pin, slips through a crack in the sky and so, passing through one heaven after the other, it finally reaches the highest, the last of all the heavens, and becomes a god of sorts; the geese, revived, bend their necks before him in awe, one goose after the other, and the wags, too, bow and twirl before him. He is their god. At a nod of his head, the wags turn on the man. They attack him, deride him and try to carry him off with them. How they laugh, the mockers, and how they humiliate him! But he remembers his father's prescription and bursts out laughing himself. His eyeglasses dance down to the tip of his nose. The whole attic chamber helps him laugh. The mockers, their own laughter drowned out, become serious. Grumbling, they climb onto ladder-like structures, which disappear along with them. Still laughing, the doctor sends them packing with a crude curse which he remembers from his years of wanderings on the riverbanks. This is how it must be: man must laugh at the powers that deride him. Luckily, he does not see his father's demons. Gradually, the mockers despair of him. What of the others, the tormentors? If they come, he will

16

not seek refuge from them in a madhouse. The new society, the Children's Republic, will drive them away. There will be no more tormentors, neither the ones that hide behind the backs of men, nor their minions who work for them out in the open.

As a rule it is in his attic chamber that his great ideas come to him. He jots them down with his pencil, with stenographic brevity, on scraps of paper. Many of his ideas have been lost, for although he knows them very well upstairs, he cannot always decipher his nervous scribblings downstairs, in his "glass cage," his cubicle flanked by the boys' dormitory on the right and the girls' dormitory on the left. Here, the other-worldly must clothe itself in this-worldly garments of reality. He spends long nights in his glass cubicle, writing essays long and short, and books which combine seriousness with humor. His style is either journalistic or sensitively sharp, almost expressionistic, though the literati describe him, Korczak, as an offspring of the "Young Poland" movement.

Tall, dark-eyed Stefa, his principal assistant, has returned from her night rounds. A flashlight in her hand, she bends over little cots, straightens a blanket here, a pillow there, breathing a soft kiss on a little head, hand or foot peeking out beneath the coverlets. Often, she and the doctor make the night rounds together. Sometimes, this makes her happy, but there are times when she becomes terribly depressed if, on such occasions, Korczak talks to her about "our" children.

"Our children" . . . God, it is just an empty phrase. This man has cast a spell upon her. How long has she been living under one roof with him? She fell in love with his dream—because of him. She is the mother of the children, and he is their father, but this father has not married the mother. They are friends, they call each other by their given names, but he is a strange man, that Henryk. Is he conceited? Does he want to remain a god-figure to her? No, he has too much wit and self-deprecation to be conceited, or to play God, or to act the mortal frozen in the majesty of his own genius. His ambition is to be a spiritual proletarian, a proletarian who has conceived a world-embracing, world-redeeming idea: "Children of all lands, unite!" Never—during all their long years together has he failed to show her tender friendship, but that friendship can never change into intimacy as between a man and a woman. He will put his arm around her or give her a fatherly kiss. He asks her advice, listens to her reports, tells her of his plans, and he shows great respect for her opinions about the problems of the children's home, which he views as the nucleus of the future state to be based upon a child's sense of justice. She will never forget how he asked the orphan boys and girls to elect twenty-two representatives to the children's parliament. He had stood before them and solemnly requested the first session of the world's first children's parliament to come to order. The meeting had taken place in the big hall; he had sat in front of the twenty-two little deputies behind a table covered with a cloth of green baize, a chairman's bell at his right hand. His short beard had glistened with a triumphant sheen, his fingers had trembled with joy like those of a miser counting his treasure. She had asked him why he had taken the chairmanship for himself. Should he not have permitted the children to elect a chairman from among their own? He had laughed aloud. "Do you think I don't care for honors? If that is what you think of me, then you certainly don't regard me as a great man. For the greater the man, the greater his craving for honors, even if they come only from children. And as for you, I wouldn't exactly become your enemy if you would start referring to me as Mr. Chairman or at least as Mr. Director-General, instead of calling me just plain Henryk." But then he had turned serious again and begun to explain to her how a revolution that was to benefit a lower class must be proclaimed and led by people coming from a different class. Accordingly, the leader of the children's revolution, too, could not be a child himself. It was the duty of the grownups to guide the children and to show them how justice and democracy, individual and society, had to be molded into one integrated whole.

Now she remembers the pride with which he had first uttered the word "pedocracy"—government by the children. A sophisticated, make-believe word? Not when *he* said it.

Now he is sitting in his glass cage, his bald head in his hands. Stefa softly knocks at the door and enters on her tiptoes. He points to the chair beside him. At first, neither of them speaks.

Later, when the silence becomes too heavy, he begins to talk. Quietly, so as not to wake the children, he tells her that, right here in Warsaw, on Krochmalna Street, he is dreaming of a huge auditorium in New York, where delegations of children from every part of the world have gathered. It is the first International Children's Congress. The children are performing one of his own plays on this occasion, and night after night people from every land and nation come to see the performance. The play depicts the transfer of authority from the grownups to the child class, and tells how these, the new rulers of the world, will introduce a new, genuine justice, the justice that dwells within each child from the moment of his birth until it is stunted by the grownup world. The grownups are beginning to understand that it is not the children who must learn from the grownups but the grownups who must learn from the children. And he, the doctor, sees himself seated in this vast auditorium, which is circular, symbolizing the terrestrial globe; he sees before him people of all nations and all races, the stage, and the performance. He can feel the pulse of all mankind.

"Would you take me with you?" Stefania asks.

He pats her hand. "Do you mean to New York?"

"Certainly. Where else?"

It was only a fatherly caress. She excuses herself—she has had a difficult day— and leaves the room. As she lies in bed, exhausted, she begins to think—as she has done Heaven knows how many times before—about their relationship. She knows that people are gossiping about her. Her own family is talking about her. Why can't they live together openly as husband and wife? It does not occur to anyone that they are not already living together in the way of a man and a woman. And yet it is so. She means nothing to him as a woman. True, he has told her of his fear that if he were ever to have children of his own flesh and blood, they might become victims—as he puts it—of his tainted heredity. But then their relationship does not necessarily have to produce children. After all, he is a doctor, and who should know better than he what can happen if one refuses to give in to the tyranny of the sex glands? Could he be a sexual deviate? No; it would not be a secret very long if he were. Does he live like a monk? Certainly he did not do so when he was young, when he acted the part of the literary Bohemian and spent whole nights prowling through side streets and alleys with disreputable companions in long capes. He himself relishes telling the story how his mother came into his room late one morning to awaken him and chided him, "Is that how you want to become a doctor—staying out all night long?" He had rubbed his eyes and mumbled sleepily, "Me? A doctor? I thought I'm studying to become a lush."

But all that was so long ago. He had gone through a great deal since then. It is not so easy to become a Janusz Korczak. Today he is even greater than people think, but he himself would be the last person to boast of his greatness. He is at once proud and humble. The older he gets, the more of a child he becomes. But it is a new breed of a child. He radiates so much purity! And whatever he says, be it important or of no particular consequence, it is truth, the most genuine, honest truth.

She leaps from her bed. At last she understands: This man is a saint! But who is a saint? No one knows that, just as no one knows the reason why one Englishman grew up to be William Shakespeare.

She sinks back onto her bed as if a hand had pushed her back, buries her head in her pillow, trying to shut out an entirely new thought. Obviously, the whole thing is much simpler. She would be able to attract him if only she were prettier. He is the way he is. But a saint? Why, the very thought would make him laugh aloud! All of world history would have turned out differently if only Cleopatra's nose would have been just a little uglier. She cannot remember who said that to her. But she knows that her own story, the life of Stefania Wilczynska, would have turned out differently if only her nose would have been just a little prettier. In such matters, all men are alike, from Janusz Korczak to Antony the ragpicker. She is younger than Korczak, but what will become of her? She is already an old maid, begging for crumbs of affection here and there—a beggar for a little love.

Eventually, she falls asleep. Tomorrow will be another working day.

21

3. BETWEEN WORLD VISION AND SWASTIKA

The years pass swiftly. Children come and grow up. When they are fourteen, they leave. They scatter all over the world and write nostalgic letters. Their places are taken by new children. Every child personifies a new hope, and all the children together stand for Korczak's ever-present dream of so many years—the emergence of a new type of man. This dream is cherished, and not only on Krochmalna Street, not only by the little Sruliks, Mosheles, Hayeles and Sarales. This man with naive wisdom written upon his narrow face, with sadness and irony hidden behind his glasses, may have doubts about many things, but not about the future of the child class from which will rise a state based on a new kind of justice. Children come and children go, but the seed he has sown remains and will bear fruit. Both Jewish and non-Jewish children will form the cornerstone of the new, lofty human edifice that will arise. The fame of the architect spreads with each passing year; this alone is the surest sign that everyone is watching the progress of the work and is eagerly awaiting the completion of the structure which he is slowly putting together, composed not only of little Sruliks and Sarales but also of Janeks and Malgosias. For by now there is a Polish orphanage in Pruszkow, where Korczak is also the spiritual father.

Children from every land, every nation and every race will join hands. They will be transformed into one single World-Child, who will transfigure and exalt the grownups.

Now, Janusz Korczak happens to be a Jew. Janusz Korczak—how many people are aware that his name appears in the Register of Jewish Generations as Hersh Goldszmit? He himself has yet to feel the sigh of generations past which lurks within his blood stream, a sigh completely unlike the sibilant, lordly quality of the Polish language. He does not know that within him, within his almost ridiculous non-elegance which is accepted as the affectation of a celebrity, there dwells the befitting poverty of a plain and simple Jew, Hersh the Glazier, his maternal grandfather, who, when he had drawn the lucky number in a lottery, had kept the news from his family so that he might remain the same old Hersh the Glazier. Korczak was named after him. But although Polish mothers consult him as the greatest child specialist and educational reformer Poland has ever produced, and although he will never exchange so much as one splash from the River Vistula for all the waters of the Danube, the Seine and the Thames, and although Mickiewicz's[2] *Pan Tadeusz* is his *Illiad*, his love for Poland will never allow him to forget the rest of the world. For in addition to being a grandson of Hersh the Glazier, he is also a grandson of a country doctor, an intellectual with a stovepipe hat and two-pointed beard, who had taken care never to forget the German he had learned, particularly Moses Mendelssohn's classic German translation of the Bible.

As the years go by, he sees that anti-Semitism is on the rise everywhere. But he does not notice that his relationship with the Polish children's home in Pruszkow is no longer so close as it used to be. The fact that he was born a Jew is exposed bit by bit, as if that were a disgrace. The force which defines the path of the Jews among the nations has willed it that his dream should glance off the Janeks, Franeks and Marishkas like a rubber ball bounces off the wall of a fortress. Only much later will he come to realize that he will have to confine his dream to children of his own race, who are thrice pitiable and

2. Adam Mickiewicz, (1798–1855), greatest romantic poet of Poland.

thrice orphaned; first, because they have no home; secondly, because, being children, they are in bondage to the grownups even if both their parents are alive and wealthy, and finally because they belong to a people which walks forever as a tormented orphan among the nations of the earth.

But he is not the kind of man who can change overnight. The words of the Prophets thunder forth to him from a Polish Bible. He has written all his books in Polish, and he speaks Polish with the children on Krochmalna—though he has nothing against their Yiddish, the language of his grandfather Hersh the Glazier, especially so because those who dislike Yiddish are the people he himself hates: the so-called "better society." He himself knows so little about Yiddish that when one of his orphans said to him in the course of a Yiddish conversation, "I'm sad," using the Polish word *smutno*, he was delighted that Polish and Yiddish were so closely related. He thought that "smutno" was a Yiddish word, and he constructed a philosophy based on his "discovery."

He draws consolation from his hope that better times cannot be far off. Someday those who began to hate him when they found out that his real name was Goldszmit will think of him again as Korczak, the Pole. After all, people still read his writings and attend his lectures. Everyone knows that it was he who discovered the world-redeeming powers of the child. In the end, the light will go forth from poor, Jewish Krochmalna Street. Eventually, all good examples will gain the respect they deserve. Here, on Krochmalna Street, children's humanity, children's justice and children's self-government still reign supreme. Here are a court of justice, a parliament, and a newspaper, all run by children. The children manage their own affairs. He, Korczak, along with

24

Stefa and their assistants, merely act as supervisors.
Small beginnings? Never mind. There is a great goal
waiting. Some day a sorely wounded, despairing world,
tired of savage grownup-ness, will come here to shabby
Krochmalna Street and will learn from the thrice-
orphaned Jewish child how to break the might of the
non-humans who keep men captive in their mousetraps
with the help of their human minions. The wags, the
mockers, and those savage tormentors from whom his
father fled to the madhouse will vanish like mice scurry-
ing off into their holes.

> Orphan boys and girls, so dreamy pale,
> Children of the race that gave to the world
> The Song of Songs and the Book of Lamentations;
> You children of Gensia, Smocza, Stawki and Niska,
> Wolynska Street and Mila—
> (The very names sound like a prayer);
> You children from cellars and basements,
> Small shoots springing up amidst the ruins:
> Sound forth the call to all the other children,
> To follow your lead and build up a world
> That will sing forth from you
> Like pure music—
> And to create the new Republic.

To create the new Republic . . . But pray, keep in
mind, Doctor, that after almost 30 years of existence on
Krochmalna Street, this home has yet to turn out its first
specimen of the new race, and that when your children
go out into the world, they come face to face with the
facts of life. Reality harnesses them to its age-old blight,
and your home remains in their memories only as a mir-
age in the wilderness of the world.

Hitler's shadow has spread over the fields of Poland

25

against the setting sun of humanity. Poland's rulers are
out hunting with fat Hermann Goering in the woods of
Bialowieza. And everywhere, the hiss of hatred: *Zhid-
zhid, zhid-zhid*. Those whose very names the hand of a
Jew would shudder to record on paper make bold to
attack the Jews—and God. The swastika has opened its
maw, and tell me, Goldszmit, what is your doddering,
fairytale children's state compared to the swastika em-
pire?

Goldszmit, Jew that you are, how can you go on sitting
in such a world smithing your gold?

4. IN THE LAND OF ISRAEL

He has been there too . . . It is a rest day and two
men are taking a walk near kibbutz Eyn Harod. One of
them is a member of the kibbutz, who hails from Poland;
the other is a visitor, Dr. Goldszmit, better known as
Korczak, a man immersed in his thoughts, grave, slightly
bent, with threads of white in his short, thin beard. He
walks softly, as if he were ashamed to tread upon the
Jewish soil.

"I remember," the visitor says, "a discussion I once
had with Itzhak Grünbaum[3] when we were students together. He wanted Zion to be the whole world, while I
wanted the whole world to be Zion."

"And in your opinion, which of you was right?" the
kibbutznik inquires.

"Which one of us was right? Both of us were. How-

3. Grünbaum (1879–1970), was a Zionist leader and one of the principal
spokesmen of Polish Jewry between the two World Wars. Settling in Palestine
in 1933, he was a signer of Israel's Declaration of Independence in 1948 and
served as Minister of the Interior in Israel's first Cabinet.

ever, as long as the world will not be Zion but only a pigsty, Zion will have to be the world."

He looks about, as if searching for something, then continues:

"I would like to build, in Jerusalem, a monument to the Unknown Orphan. But that would be only a symbol. What I would really like to establish in Jerusalem is a World Center of Spirituality. After all, the human spirit, too, is an orphan in this world. Don't you agree? Also, the first International Children's Congress should be in Jerusalem, not in New York. But then I'm only—"

He wants to crack a joke about himself, but he only makes a deprecating gesture with his hand. "Never mind."

The ground is thick with tall blades of grass, rising on their tiptoes, lifting their thin necks to the visitor. He stops and looks. Did he know them generations ago? Were they blades of grass then, too, or were they something else?

He walks away from the kibbutznik for a moment, turns off into the grass and almost gets lost in the green expanse. Then he emerges again and looks around in surprise as if he had just stepped out from remote antiquity.

The harsh scream of a bird. That scream, too, is from the distant past.

"On my travels through this land," he tells the kibbutznik, "I saw a lonely tree descending from a bare, sloping hill. So, too, a prophet might have descended from the barren mountains with his message to the people in the valley below."

Suddenly, the mockers are upon him, putting out their tongues. They have not been around for quite some time. And now they are here, of all places! A wind begins to blow, an *Eretz Yisrael* wind, and the evil inheritance flees from the heritage of antiquity which is coming alive again in a new form.

He falls silent, then murmurs to himself:

"Fancies! Idle fancies!"

It occurs to him that he wants to ask his kibbutznik friend a question.

"If there is a God, what do you think He is?"

"A *halutz*," his companion replies.

"My trouble," says Korczak, "is that I'm still a *goy*. It's not easy for me to become like you. If any of the things you are saying had been written, or could have been written, by Slowacki, Hoene-Wronski[4] or Wyspianski,[5] then, my *landsman*, I would be reciting it to you in Polish and it would have been poetry, philosophy, or Polish culture. But in Poland they have other ideas about God. Slowacki says that God loves power, that He loves wild horses and refuses to tame them. Nietzscheanism even before Nietzsche. Nietzsche was also of Polish origin—Nitzki, you know. As for me, I hate wild horses; I'm afraid of them. What if a wild horse should trample a child to death? If God really is as Slowacki pictures Him, then I would have to hate both God and Slowacki. I'm still a *goy*, my friend—I mean, a Pole—but I am beginning to feel more and more like a grandson of Hersh the Glazier. And Hersh the Glazier certainly must have been afraid of wild horses."

5. BACK ON KROCHMALNA STREET

Krochmalna 92. It is night. To the left and to the right, the children are asleep. The doctor is sitting in his

4. Jozef Hoene-Wronski (1778–1853), Polish mystic philosopher.
5. Stanislaw Wyspianski (1869–1907), Polish dramatist in verse.

glass-partitioned cubicle, writing to his friends in a kib-butz after his second—and last—visit to the Land of the Jews. "I am an old man and tortured more and more by the blunt hatred of those in whose language I was raised. Let me be honest: there still are some who stand up for Janusz Korczak, the Pole. They feel that Goldszmit is just a curiosity. But the majority feels otherwise, and now I know that the majority is right. What could give me back my strength? Jerusalem the Eternal City, or a verdant kibbutz. But how? If I were younger and, par-ticularly, if I would be able to take my children there with me. My life here has ceased to be my life. Some-times I feel as if I were seated in a private box in a cosmic theater, somewhere in outer space, and looking down through my opera glasses at a devil's opera that is being performed on the planet Earth below. But all that takes only minutes, you understand, I, too, am part of the opera.

"There are two things that keep me here: the respon-sibility for my children, and the memories I have left of an old-young soil, of a sun which once shone upon the Prophets and now shines upon the *halutzim*. Sometimes I dream of a little room in Jerusalem with a small table—and on that table, a Hebrew dictionary, some paper, and a pencil. Sometimes I am in Tiberias, in a small prayer room, a silent Jew: no one knows from where I came and no one knows what I need. Sometimes I am even high up on Mount Carmel, silhouetted against the wide open skies, the open expanse, the open sea—there is my orphanage, flown over from Warsaw on the wings of birds without immigration permits. Who cares about the British? Or the Mandatory authorities? I hear the song of birds whose names I do not know. My chil-dren have new names. Those are my dreams. But now it is too late.

"There is an abyss between Jewish children and Polish children. I would like to close that abyss, but it is too late. The workers of the world did not unite during the First World War, nor did they unite afterwards. Now a second world war is coming, and new chasms, deep trenches, are being dug everywhere. It is too late; still, I hope that someday the Children's International will arise.

"My friends, I am an old sick Jew, but I am dreaming of new works to write. I have a whole list of titles: *The Travels of Hershek, Little King David the Second, Children of the Bible*, and so forth. All these stories will be about the Jewish child in the Land of the Jews. . . . The English will not rule over you forever . . . We here are living tombstones, while you have baby carriages, a future, a future. . . . At night I dream about so many things. . . . Sometimes I talk with my friend from the planet Ro, an old wise philosopher named Zi. He comforts me: The earth is still young, he says; that's why it is so wild. . . . When it will get to be as old as the planet Ro, everything will be different on your planet Earth. . . . And it is Jerusalem, I say to the old philosoper Zi from the planet Ro, that will show the way. . . . How would it be, my friends (one can dream, can one not?), if I had a room not far from, let us say, K'far Giladi, not large, on a flat roof with transparent walls so that I could look up at your stars while I do my writing at night? You are seeking, with toil and righteousness, to communicate with the earth . . . In time, you will also be able to communicate with heaven . . .

"I do not remember whether I have already written to you about this before: now of all times, when it is too late, I have designed a new flag for my children's home. It is only half as big as the flag of little Matthew, the child whom, in my imagination, I have made the ruler. My present hero is a little wanderer in exile whom I call by my own name, my real name. That little wanderer, Hershek, represents the transmigration of the soul of a boy from the Bible, with a ruddy complexion and beautiful eyes, a boy who fought against Goliath and then reigned over Israel and sang hymns to God. However, my world vision still endures.

"But now back to the flag. It is the flag of Matthew, and of Hershek, too. But it will be Hershek, not Matthew, who will raise it. One side of the flag will be green. On it, there will be chestnut blossoms, the brightest meadow green. This will symbolize the World-Child. On the other side, a star of David the color of the sea, against a background of joyous white. You know what *that* symbolizes. What else will there be? Nothing else. All this was written by a doctor of medicine who knows that he is suffering from a serious disease of the heart."

6. THE GESTAPO

Fate willed it that Korczak was forced to put on a brand-new uniform. He was drafted into the Polish army as a reserve officer. But before long he was back with the children and Stefa, because the swastika flag had been raised over Warsaw. The children's home had been evicted from its three-story building on Krochmalna Street. Korczak had to wear his new uniform without epaulets, and soon the uniform was no longer new. It looked as miserable as a Jew in the ghetto. Korczak laughed at the ghetto, at the uniform, at himself and at this world that bred Hitlers. When he wore that uniform, it was easier for him to get bread, potatoes and a little sugar for his children's home. Such was the power of the uniform. He has tried to picture for himself what the Nazis would look like without their uniforms. He has even said to Stefa: "Foolish girl, how is it that you haven't managed to get yourself a uniform as yet?"

But this time no amount of joking will help—though he sometimes tries to pretend he does not know it.

Gestapo headquarters. A huge building on Szuch Avenue. This is not the first time he has been summoned to report there. The creatures who are rampant there are not mere mockers who drive people mad, who are out to bewilder others, to drag them into chaos or to turn man in a victim of a pinhead. They are the tormentors, the murderers, the most ruthless foes of mortal man. There they have their way. There, in joyous friendship, they collaborate with their living uniformed minions, the servants of the swastika. His poor father had tried to escape by entering a mental hospital, for even in his time the world had already jumped its shaft like a wild horse. That is why his madness had reflected a little of the truth of days to come. Man is forever under siege. Forever.

Now, as he walks to Gestapo headquarters, he can still hear his father's terrified cries: "There they are! Look! There they are!"

Yes, there they are, ordering the living doers of their will to conquer and exterminate the world. Among these minions there is no lack of people from the so-called intelligentsia who have come to thirst after blood. They are graduates of universities and can quote from world classics; they have written books, produced paintings and composed music of their own. The Nazi who has been assigned to supervise the children's home had been a pediatrician himself in civilian life. He is a tall German in a Gestapo uniform with a green velvet collar, and as tall and thin as he is, so thick and fat are the cigars that reek from between his lips. He seems to be torturing his cigars, not puffing them. Let us call him Doctor Von Blutenau. This long-legged Nazi was able to lace his talk with such erudite expressions as "categorical imperative." Furthermore, it turned out that this German, the former pediatrician, knew all about Korczak's theory, as he called it, and with the same irony that dripped from the form of address, "My respected colleague," which he used in speaking to Korczak, he spoke of the Children's Republic of which that "respected colleague" was the president. The theory of self-government for children is false and corrupt, just like the Jews, and if you go to visit the republic at its present home you can see the consequences.

Such is the Gestapo man to whom Dr. Korczak is about to report.

When Korczak arrived at the building on Szuch Avenue, Dr. Von Blutenau again addressed him as "My respected colleague." He even deigned to remark: "We're both academicians, are we not?" and offered him a seat. Then Dr. Blutenau said to him, "Why, my respected colleague, you're a Jewish pig!" "Respected colleague" and "Jewish pig"—Korczak could not help laughing at the combination.

The German gave him a stern look. Nobody was supposed to laugh in his presence. But Korczak's sense of humor had been aroused. Who knew? It might not help, but there certainly was no harm in trying. So he began to tell jokes from his student days. Memories of his father stirred within him and, without knowing it, he imitated his father's grimaces. His artistic imagination stood him in good stead now. He recited odd and humorous passages from his play, *The Madmen's Senate*, which Stefan Jaracz had produced at the Atheneum Theater. The German did not laugh because he did not want to laugh. He yawned, stretched out his long, stork-like legs under his desk, meditated for a little while, and finally said, "You have a good crooked Jewish head."

That was intended as a Nazi compliment of sorts. There was a reason why, with cold irony and with epithets added from the Nazi vocabulary, Von Blutenau had been referring to Korczak as "My respected colleague." If the necessity arose, one could always make use of the international reputation of that Polish Jew, who, with his Slavic name, had so craftily wormed his way into the confidence of Aryan circles abroad and had been acknowledged by them as a great thinker and reformer. By that time Dr. Von Blutenau already knew that the Warsaw ghetto was going to be liquidated and that children in Korczak's *donnerkreuz-verdammte* Children's Republic of Jewish swindlers was not going to last much longer. Ha, ha, ha! their leader was still running about in the ghetto, scrounging for groceries for his children. Why, he really seemed to believe that this so-called Children's Republic would survive Der Fuehrer's Thousand-Year Reich! At the same time, Dr. Von Blutenau was sure that this Goldszmit Jew, with all the damned autosuggestion at his command, would grab at any straw to remain alive and that, at the last moment, he would turn in those filthy rascals, those negroid Jew-brats, and betray his own—excuse the expression—his own idea as well. For the price of a dirty little bit of life the Jew would confirm everything he would be told to confirm to the foreigners, and deny everything he would be told to deny. That's how the Jews are, the whole lot of them! Ha, ha! That's what they are like! Heil Hitler!

He informed Korczak that he and his children would have to move immediately to the little ghetto. Korczak bowed his head.

"I see you are sad because you are about to lose your territory," Dr. Blutenau sneered. "You Jews are doing very well in the ghetto. You manage to adjust to every situation, but you don't know how good you have it. You are never satisfied. You are like a man who is sorry because he has no golden shoes to wear but doesn't know that he will soon have both his legs cut off."

7. ON THE EVE OF EXTERMINATION

The Jews were standing in the streets of the Warsaw ghetto studying the posters announcing the "resettlement." There was a lively exchange of comments. After all, they consoled each other, Warsaw was still Warsaw, the heart of Jewish Poland, and it was entirely different from all the other ghettoes. It was all very clear: Only those who were considered "useless" would be sent to work for the Germans "somewhere in the East." It was simply inconceivable that the Warsaw ghetto might be liquidated. It so happened that next to the poster announcing the impending "resettlement" there was another poster bearing the words, "The Road to Happiness." It was an advertisement for a new Yiddish play which was going to be performed in the ghetto.

Once again, Korczak was called to report to Gestapo headquarters on Szuch Avenue. He was still wearing his threadbare uniform because he had nothing better to put on. His legs were swollen and they hurt him, but he was not going to use some starved ghetto Jew as his riksha man. True, he had a bad heart. But did that give him special privileges? What was so unusual about a ghetto Jew having trouble with his heart?

He walked on and stopped, walked a little more and stopped again. From time to time he leaned against a wall to rest. Somehow, he dragged himself to the building where Von Blutenau had ordered him to report. Von Blutenau was friendly—like a hangman.

"This conversation will be confidential. Do you under-stand? Strictly confidential."

"I understand."

"Of course you understand. After all, my respected colleague, you are an intelligent Jewish shit. Well, lis-ten: The Third Reich is fed up with the parasites in the Warsaw ghetto, and with the children in your cesspool, Mister Jew, in your so-called Children's Republic. There are quite a few of them—two hundred! Correct? Para-sites, that's what they are! Or, to be more exact, insects, according to your own Karl Marx, the one with the rab-binical beard. Marx said that the Jews have squeezed into the cracks of the Polish economy like certain insects. They are vermin, all of them. And you know how people deal with vermin, don't you? As for you, my respected Jew colleague, we can put you to good use for certain purposes. *Jawohl!* We have already indicated as much to you before. Do you want to live or don't you? Yes, or no? Time is short."

Something flashed behind Korczak's spectacles.

"Of what possible use could an insect be to you?"

"We need one insect who will tell the foreigners that those stories about our killing vermin are not true. We have other plans for you, too."

Korczak rose from his chair. Without a word, he moved toward the door.

Von Blutenau leaped to his feet. "The day will come when you will kiss my hands, you Jewish shit! Not even a bedbug wants to be squashed."

He savored the last sentence as if it had been a gem of wisdom. He was so pleased that he flicked his whip over his own boots.

He fairly danced back to his desk, leaned back in his chair and began to clean his fingernails.

8. REVOLT AND DEBATE

Korczak locked himself in his little room at the new quarters of his orphanage. He called it his "isolation chamber." From time to time he addressed himself to an invisible partner as if to seek advice.

On that day Stefa had happened to talk with one of those who knew the truth about the impending "resettlement." These people had managed to escape from the German slaughter in the countryside and to make their way into the Warsaw ghetto. They knew that "resettlement" meant Treblinka, and that Treblinka was a place of death from which there was no escape. The ghetto was sealed off so tightly that not even a fly could be smuggled out of the ghetto into the Aryan sector of the city. And not only the Warsaw ghetto was going to be liquidated; the Germans had decided to liquidate the entire Jewish people once and for all.

Stefa burst into the doctor's "isolation chamber" with Abrasha, a palefaced boy with dark eyes and beetling eyebrows. Stefa's face was stern and there was a defiant look in her eyes. Abrasha was her pet, and the doctor's, too. More than once she had hugged, kissed and caressed him; it seemed to her that in this way the kisses which Abrasha had received from the doctor would be transferred to her. She liked to pretend that she herself had given birth to Abrasha, that she and the doctor were his real parents. Now it was no longer "our children" but "our *child*."

Nobody knew where Abrasha had come from. Somehow he was as if he had been born an orphan. The only clue to his origin was his name, Abrasha; his parents had, in all likelihood, come to Warsaw from Lithuania.

Both he and Stefa were rebels. Abrasha talked like an adult. His beetling eyebrows looked like one thick,

37

angry arch of hair. He and the other children, he said, should have been taught how to use a gun and to fight back. Instead, they had been lulled into foolish games; they had been taught to play at children's courts of justice and children's parliaments. They had been told about a children's republic. They had put out a children's newspaper, they had produced plays, and they had been made to believe that they were the pioneers of a new world. Oh yes, the doctor and his assistants had seen to it that the children were healthy and clean, and that they had enough exercise. The children had also studied school subjects. Before the ghetto days, they had made trips, sung hiking songs and spent several weeks at camp each summer. That was all very nice, but what good had it done them? Instead of learning how to be just they should have learned how to be strong and how to handle a gun.

"We'll all be killed, the children and the grownups!" Stefa cried out. "Do you really believe there will be anyone left alive whom we could beg for a few potatoes or a little sugar?"

The doctor smiled wrily.

"Did you come to lecture me?" he asked, turning to her, "or do you have some concrete suggestion?"

"Yes! I do have a suggestion! Let's close up this boarding school. Let's tell the children the truth: we can no longer offer them any shelter. Tell me: If just one or two of them will be able to escape and survive, wouldn't it be worth while?"

"To survive. . . . Do you believe in miracles?"

"No, but in a world of blind chance, in a world that no longer makes any sense, even this could happen."

"Do you realize that this would mean leaving our children on their own to fend for themselves?"

"Your God has left everybody on his own to fend for himself."

"We must accept responsibility for all our children until the very end. Besides, supposing we were to tell the children a hundred times over that the boarding school is closing up, do you believe that they'd listen to us and go? Well, they won't. They'll never leave. Not ever."

"I would like to join the underground youth organization; they are planning to resist," said Abrasha, lowering his eyes. "But then, what weapons do they have? One revolver; nothing more. Sure, someday they'll get more revolvers, bullets and hand grenades, but by that time I—we—none of us will be alive any more. Besides, how could I leave the Doctor, or Miss Stefa, or my friends? No, I can't leave!"

The doctor hugged Abrasha. "I still have some friends left in the Aryan sector," he said. "They have sent me forged Aryan papers, but I let them know a long time ago that I will never use these documents. I will not run away from the ghetto like a rat from a sinking ship. I will stay with my children until the end. But—tell me, my son: supposing a miracle were to happen and we would get some weapons, what good would that do us now?"

"If we had guns and we'd hear the Germans shouting in the courtyard, '*Juden, 'raus,*'[6] none of us would listen to them. They'd have to come up and get us themselves. I and the other children, the older ones and the ones with the most courage, would open fire on them and then we . . . we would die with dignity."

The doctor sighed.

"I understand, my son. I understand."

Then, turning to Stefa, he said. "Listen to me, Stefa.

6. "All Jews, out!"

You of all people should know that I am not a believer in Tolstoy. Do you remember Mickiewicz's *Ode to Youth*? We all had to learn it by heart when we were young.

" 'Violence must be met with violence!' There was a time when I, too, was a fighter. When I was young, I served some time at the Pawiak Prison. . . . Haven't I taught our children that the struggle for justice is a two-fold one—a fight not only for ourselves but also for the others? Haven't I taught them that, and haven't I told them that all of life is a battle and that we will have to reshape life so that it will cease to be a battle?"

"But that is impossible!" Abrasha interrupted. Again, he was talking like a grown man. "It's impossible! We should have been taught one thing only: how to be soldiers, good soldiers. Has it occurred to the doctor, even at this stage, to think about weapons?"

"I've been to the Aryan sector, to see my friends. . . . I wasn't able to accomplish anything. All they did was offer me shelter. 'You we will hide; after all, you are a Pole.' Nothing more. By the way, who taught you all these ideas? Was it Miss Stefa?"

Stefa's voice rose to a near scream.

"You wanted a great cause, but you are bankrupt. You should have realized from the very start that even justice must have guns!"

"Maybe so. . . . But do you know how justice is created? Why, with more justice!" said Korczak with the sorrow of a loser coupled with the firmness of one sure of himself. "Yes, that's how it is, my child."

Stefa felt his fatherly tone like a stab at her heart. What manner of "child" did he take her for? Like Abrasha, except that she was wearing a dress?

"Henryk." She talked quickly, looking not into his face but at some point beyond him. "For thirty years and more, I have followed wherever you led. But *that* is not the way people really behave."

"There comes a time when even the most beautiful dreams turn into nonsense," Abrasha cut in.

"Did Miss Stefa teach you that?" the doctor asked quietly, as if he had been accused of some crime.

"No, Doctor. Life has taught me that."

Abrasha felt hurt. He had never read the children's newspaper, and hardly ever accepted election to the children's parliament or to the children's court. He was a precocious youngster, a loner, and had written things which he never showed to anyone.

"So you are saying that it was all madness?" the doctor demanded. His voice was hoarse. "Very well. But I am mad enough to believe that this madness was more important than all the realities."

Stefa leaped to her feet. "What could be more important than reality?" she flared.

"Perhaps we should stop this discussion," said Korczak, with an absent-minded laugh.

His absent-mindedness hurt Stefa. She had tried to restrain herself, to become softer, but now there was too much turmoil within her.

Abrasha quietly left the room. He no longer felt like a rebel; all that remained was a feeling of guilt. The doctor was an old, sick man. What could he do? Turn back the clock of his life? He was doomed, just like all the others.

The silence between Korczak and Stefa was long and painful. It was Stefa who finally broke it.

"Henryk," she began. "I sympathize with you, but I stopped understanding you a long time ago."

Korczak winked at her. "Well, if that is so, then I must be a great man. Emerson said that to be great means to be misunderstood."

"You've become superstitious, Henryk."

41

"So I've become a reactionary? And what's wrong with that?"

"You are a scientist. You used to hate religious prejudices. You used to make fun of fanaticism, mysticism and things like that. You used to be progressive. It didn't disturb me when you would recite the Mourner's—what do you call it—the Mourner's Kaddish—with the children. It sounded funny. It was not my taste. You know I am an agnostic, but I understood: Pedagogy, tolerance, and all that. What do children understand of such things? They want to have the Kaddish recited in memory of their parents. Very well. But how can you explain why you observed Yom Kippur last year? When did you become such a devout Jew?"

"A devout Jew?" Korczak repeated the question. "Who? Me?"

"So you're *not* a devout Jew?" Stefa demanded. "What are you, then—a hypocrite?"

"Neither the one nor the other."

"I can understand you less and less. You were swaying at your prayers like an old, primitive Jew. You raised your arms and screamed to high heaven. How odd! Did Spinoza also scream to God, I would like to know? I thought that your God was the God of Spinoza."

"There was a time when I believed in Spinoza's pantheistic concept of God. But now I have come to understand that God is either something that truly exists—a person, a super-person—or else He is nothing, absolutely nothing. He cannot be reduced to a formula."

"Absolutely correct, Henryk. He is nothing, absolutely nothing."

"Your certainty, my dear, is so shallow that it almost appears to be deep."

"Thanks for the compliment. I have read your *Prayers for Unbelievers*. Now let me tell you something, Doctor

Goldszmit; it's all just literature. What kind of talk is that? 'O God, I love Thee for having created such an interesting world—the solar system and the bedbug, the potato and Sir Isaac Newton.' I don't remember the whole thing any more, but you said something to that order. However, you lost sight of the most important fact. You say that God created both bedbugs and solar systems. Nonsense! The trouble is that He created absurd contrasts: a Henryk Goldszmit on the one hand and an international bandit, Hitler, on the other. Created, I say? Why, He neither exists, nor did He ever create anything. I don't see God anywhere. All I see is Nazis. So I am asking you again: to whom did you raise your arms on Yom Kippur? To whom did you cry out? And before that, why did you make a Seder last Passover? Are you fool enough to believe that there was someone in heaven listening to you? And what did you want with all the Vedas and Zend-Avestas on your table?"

"I am now a man who has no more alternatives, Stefa; I've nothing left to choose from. If God were a Spinozan formula, such a God could very well have permitted Nazis to exist. But the God of all the Vedas is also not for me. It may be poetry, philosophy, but it is not God. And what if He would *not* exist—that personal God of my grandfather, Hersh the Glazier? Why, then the Nazis would be right! Now, mind you, I'm not saying that the God of Hersh the Glazier exists for sure. I simply don't know. I am not a theologian—although in my blood I am, in fact, a theologian, just like any other Jew. You may not know it, but even you are a theologian, just blasphemously, negatively so. I'll tell you: the problem is something quite different. If He does indeed exist, then He should know each and every one of us personally. Personally, I say, without any philosophizing. We know all of our children, don't we? We know every one of them,

43

singly and separately. We feel responsible for all of them together, and for each one of them separately. But what about Him? . . . He . . ."

He stopped, and when he resumed speaking he spoke more to himself than to her:

"Mass holocausts . . . mass graves. . . . Where, then, is the responsibility for each individual? If God is not an abstraction, if He is a real God, a personal God, then each and every one of us must have his own unique destiny, just as each person has his personal measurements, his personal size . . ."

Stefa fairly went into a dance. She clapped her hands.

"But everything is a matter of supreme indifference to that personal God of yours. Mass holocausts, mass graves—history is full of them. What do they matter to Him? So on whom have you been calling? On a formula again?"

"Stefa." His voice was warm and vibrant. "I have been calling on a hypothesis. I am a skeptical believer. I don't know—but I heard someone calling from within me. Maybe it was Hersh the Glazier."

"Your grandfather was primitive and so he had a primitive God, who never really existed. But the God of the Spinozas also does not exist. And if He did, then He must have been shot by the first Nazi who came along."

She made a deprecating gesture.

She was already standing at the door when suddenly she turned back to look at him. How faded she has become, he thought, recalling the eager, vital Stefania Wilczynska of their first meeting.

Yes, they both had been young then. She had never been pretty, but there had been that vitality, that sprightliness, that dark, aggressive fire in her eyes, those sweeping gestures. Warsaw—a Warsaw backdrop in Switzerland, the park. . . . He remembered the park, the sun, such a strange sun. . . . Perhaps it had been a Swiss sun, except that to her it was Warsaw in the sun. . . .

He felt that she wanted to say something, but that she was hesitating.

"Stefa, I beg of you, don't keep any secrets from me!"

She was silent, deep in her thoughts. She was pale. She sat down heavily on a chair, and she began to talk, very fast.

"Do you know why I too, tried my luck at a kibbutz?"

"You mean the time you left the children with me . . . and with those few assistants of ours?"

"Yes, the time I ran away."

"From whom did you run away? Was it from me?"

"It was from my foolish love, which was never returned . . . You gratefully accepted the labors of my days, and I know that we are friends. But what did you know about the anguish of my nights?"

He lowered his head.

"There hasn't been even one night . . . in all those dozens of years which I gave to you and the children . . . when I would have—"

She hid her face in her tired, orphaned hands.

"When in my bed of humiliation . . ."

He looked at her out of one corner of his eye: "*What* was it you said just now?"

". . . when in my bed of humiliation, I did not give rein to erotic fantasies, like wild horses, with *you* always in the center. This happens before I fall asleep, after I fall asleep, and in my dreams. I will not even speak about my conscious thoughts of you . . . what kind of a man you are . . . And so I ran away. . . . But why am I telling you all that? I don't know why. But I feel that this is my last chance to tell you . . . to admit it. . . . Call it a confession, call it hysteria, whatever you like. . . . What

45

have I left to lose? . . . Yes, the kibbutz . . . Strange.
. . . Only there did I realize that I was lost. . . . I could
not run away from my love for you . . . or from the
children. . . . You had harnessed me to your dream. . . .
And Hitler was moving closer and closer to Poland. . . .
So how could I have left you, the children and . . . and
my failure? And so I came back. . . ."

"Your failure, you say? Yes, Stefa . . . A failure. . . .
Man is forever under siege. . . . But then, what can we
really know?"

He took off his glasses, polished them for a long time,
and said nothing more.

9. A SCENE FROM LONG AGO

After Stefa had left the room, Korczak recalled a
strange incident from his student days; the recollection
came to him unbidden, as if it had been sent to him from
somewhere far away. Sometimes things happen which
one attempts to suppress, to lock up and not let out, just
as parents keep a defective child locked up in an attic.
One can rush or weep one's whole life away without ever
realizing that one has cheated oneself of a treasure. But
sometimes it may come to pass that the door will open up
and the monster will put out his head, not looking like a
monster at all, and reveal his secret to those who have
kept him under lock and key.

And that truth, with which he had come face to face so
unexpectedly, like one suddenly meets a long-forgotten
acquaintance on a street corner, made Korczak feel
ashamed. From time to time he had told Stefa about his
personal quirks, past and present, in order to be able to
laugh at them together with her. He had told her about
everything, but not about that one. It had not entered

his mind in years; it had lain in the deep, dark bottom of his recollections. He had been hiding it from himself. Without even consciously thinking of it, he had looked upon it as a sin. He had analyzed all his other abnormalities, laughed at them, pushed them away from him, destroyed them and come out whole, exactly as he had laughed at the atavistic mocking nuisances who had been unable to resist him. For instance, after he had delivered his one-sentence speech at the students' meeting and his fellow students had laughed at him among themselves, he would walk over to such a laughing group, join in their laughter, and so put an end to the whole affair. Even in the non-human mockers there had been something at once demonic and light-headed, which had made it easier for him to pay them back in kind. But this thing . . . it had been every bit as serious as a crime. This had been different. It should never have happened, never. How can one explain sitting for hours each night in a post-mortem room, looking at the faces of dead children?

He could see it all again. It was there, before his eyes, and all at once it acquired a new meaning; a finger pointing: "Look! Look over there!"

It had happened in that other Warsaw, the Warsaw of his student days. It is late at night. Where is he? In the post-mortem room. What is he doing there so late? He sits there for hours, that young student Goldszmit, staring at the little faces of dead children. Having paid the guard for this strange pastime, he sits there and stares. What is he doing there? What is he looking for?

It is quiet. The guard has dozed off. The dead children look as if they, too, have fallen asleep. The student keeps on staring at them for hours on end. It is so strange that even the night should begin to wonder. Why is he doing this? And what kind of a stare is that?

47

Are the little faces angry? No; they look tormented, but calm. You can tell from their faces that somewhere on the other side of life these children will wake up again. Their present state is only temporary. They will move from one life into another. Until then, they are resting. There are such things as misfortune, suffering, sickness, murder, dying. But *to die is not the same as being dead*! Dying is not death!

During one of those nights the student leaped to his feet with a shout of joy:

"Dying is not death! It is not death! They all will come to life again!"

He rushes up to the guard and shakes him awake, shouting:

"Dying is not death! Not even murder is death! Where is death? You tell me! Where is death? I can't see it. It is not here. Do you hear? I discovered this all by myself, you brute! All by myself!"

The guard brushes him off like a fly. "Let me sleep, madman! The very idea—staring at dead children! I don't need your money! Get out of here!"

He relives it all over again, and he wants to see Abrasha and Stefa as soon as possible.

That evening he tells them the story.

Abrasha's lips tremble; he experiences in his own mind everything the doctor has told him. Stefa's face remains grim.

"Even assuming that this is more than just one of your imaginings," she says, "and assuming that the faces of these children gave proof that they had not been destroyed forever, what of it? Very well. Let us assume that there is no such thing as destruction. There is only eternity. Well, isn't it enough for you that such a thing as murder exists? The victims suffer, one way or the other. Even worse: if all things are eternal, then the murderer

48

must be eternal also. He only passes from one world to another. Your eternity is of the Nazi sort."

"Always the same Stefa," Korczak strokes her hand. "If there is such a thing as eternity, then there is also such a thing as God. And if there is a God, then the eternity of the murderers is their everlasting punishment."

But Stefa does not give up.

"If eternity is eternal life, then it is also eternal murder. The murderers keep on killing, even in that eternity of yours. You have taken it into your head that there is a God. Very well, assuming that there is a God, whom does He help? Hasn't He been delivering you and your kind into the hands of the Nazis?"

"Am I in His place that I should know the answer? All I'm saying is that—for me—for me this one experience from my youth is sufficient—"

"What happened after the guard threw you out as if you had been mad?"

"I buried the memory somewhere, and now it has come back to the surface. It has come to comfort me."

"Comfort is good only for children, Henryk."

"I'm not dogmatic. But I can no longer dismiss it as mere hypothesis. This is something more. It's different, I tell you. Different . . ."

"Life everlasting? But your God is supposed to be personal, and life everlasting is not a personal thing."

"I understand. I understand. That's what it's all about. But I am talking about a true experience. And again, I repeat: I don't know. But this is different. The sleep on the faces of those children was a *good* sleep. Do you understand, Stefa? It was good. It was a promise of reawakening. God, if He exists, is good. And while I have no absolute conviction, I now have a strong feeling that He . . ."

"Congratulations, Mr. Theologian, on your good Lord God," said Stefa with an angry laugh. Leaving him with Abrasha, she ran out to have a good cry. Or was she no longer capable of weeping, but only of bitter determination?

"Don't go away, Abrasha. I have something to tell you."

"I am not a philosopher," Abrasha replied, "but the story about the dead children is beautiful—even if it is—I don't know—"

"That's not what I want to talk to you about. If we must die by a murderer's hand, then let us at least have weapons. That's all very well and good. But what if one *must* die *without* weapons? Then there is still another way: to die singing. To strike back at the murderer by singing. The murderer has *got to* believe in destruction and has got to believe that the victim believes he will be destroyed forever. But if the victim begins to sing right into the murderer's face—"

"How so?"

"That's simple. They will make us march to the *Umschlagplatz*.[7] When they do, then we, from the children's home, will march in step, just as if we were going on one of our hikes: one, two, three; one, two, three. And we will sing. You know our flag, Abrasha, don't you? I want you to march right behind me, hold our flag high, and sing. All the rest of us will be singing, too. Do you understand, Abrasha?"

"If we will have to die without a fight, then we will die singing!" Abrasha shouted joyously and planted a kiss on the doctor's cheek. "Singing! Singing!"

"Oh, one thing more," said Korczak. "You know our tradition: we put on plays. We are going to put on our

---

7. Transfer point, where the deportees were loaded on trains for Treblinka.

last play. I have already decided which one. It will be *The Post Office*. It was written by a man from India named Tagore. This play teaches us not to be afraid of death. Death is not destruction. On the contrary; death is a healer. Would you like to play the leading role?"

10. THE PERFORMANCE

The Post Office, by Rabindranath Tagore. The performance is well attended. Among the guests are supporters of the orphanage, those who have been donating bread for the children, money for medicines, and so forth—the—forgive the expression—ghetto "millionaires," who before long will also be marching to the *Umschlagplatz*.

Stefa has assembled all the children. The author from India speaks through the mouths of Jewish children in the ghetto. Abrasha is playing the role of Amal, a sick boy who is not allowed to leave his room. He is looking out into the street from the window, accosting one person or another below and starting conversations. Just now he is talking with the watchman.[8]

WATCHMAN:
My gong sounds to tell the people:
Time waits for no one, but goes on forever.
AMAL-ABRASHA: Where? To what land?

— — — — — — — — — — —

Oh, I do wish to fly with time
To that land of which no one knows anything.

8. The translation of the passages quoted from Tagore's play is based partly on Aaron Zeitlin's own free Yiddish version, which differs in several points from the definitive English text published in *Collected Poems and Plays of Rabindranath Tagore*, New York, 1951, The MacMillan Co., pp. 179–200.

WATCHMAN:
All of us will have to go there one day, my child.
AMAL:
Me, too?
WATCHMAN:
Certainly!
AMAL:
But the doctor won't let me out.
WATCHMAN:
One day the doctor himself
may take you there by the hand.
AMAL:
He won't! You don't know him.
He keeps me locked up in my room.
WATCHMAN:
One doctor greater than he will come and let us free.
AMAL:
When will he come? When will
that great doctor come?

Something has happened. All the audience has left! Stefa has gathered the children and left. What about Abrasha? Where has he gone? The stage is empty.

Dr. Von Blutenau, the tall German with the cigar in his mouth, has risen to his feet. He walks straight up to Korczak and blows smoke from his cigar into the doctor's face.

"Don't you know that it is strictly forbidden for you Jews to perform plays written by Aryans? How did you dare put on a performance like that? Have you gone mad? Did you believe, with your crooked Jewish brain, that something like this could remain a secret?"

"Yes, I know." Korczak is trying to speak calmly. "There is no shortage of informers. By the way, *The Post*

Office may have been written by an Aryan, but the idea it conveys is quite Jewish."

"Is that so? Well, then, you are hereby requested to call the whole lot back in. Tell them to finish the performance. This is a command!"

Korczak goes out and returns with Stefa and the children—those who were in the audience and those who were in the cast, with Abrasha in the lead. The show goes on. Von Blutenau is listening attentively. Eventually the performance draws to a close.

This is the final scene. The sick boy no longer feels any pain. The Royal Physician enters—the good healer, who is called Death.

THE ROYAL PHYSICIAN:
Now be quiet, all of you. I'll sit by his pillow.
Sleep is coming over him. Put out the oil lamp,
and let only the starlight stream in.
Hush, he's asleep.

MADHAV, AMAL'S STEPFATHER (to the Uncle, the Gaffer):
Why are you standing there like a statue,
with folded hands? . . . What's going on here?
Why are you putting out the light in the room?
How will starlight help?

THE UNCLE:
Be quiet, unbeliever.

SUDHA, THE FLOWER GIRL:
Amal, I have come.

THE ROYAL PHYSICIAN:
He's asleep.

SUDHA:
I've brought him some flowers.
Mayn't I put them into his hand?

THE ROYAL PHYSICIAN:

He's asleep.

SUDHA:

When will he wake up?

THE ROYAL PHYSICIAN:

As soon as the king comes and calls him.

SUDHA:

Could you not whisper a word from me in his ear?

THE ROYAL PHYSICIAN:

What should I say?

SUDHA:

Tell him that Sudha has not forgotten him.

— — — — — — — — — — — — — —

Dr. Von Blutenau is applauding; it is probably an ironic gesture. He tells Korczak to take the whole rabble out of his sight. When everyone else has left, he says to Korczak:

"That boy who played Amal is gifted, but he won't be an actor for long. There must be a reason why that man from India is called Rabindranath. He really does have a rabbinic mentality. Death is nature, nature is murder. *Ergo*, death is murder. This is a true Aryan syllogism which neither you, nor that whole Jewish trash, nor even that Indian rabbi seem to understand. You want to fool your children, but it will do you no good. Death is total destruction. And yet, the fact is I want you to go on fooling the children—but in a different way than before, my respected Jew colleague. There is a rumor going about in the ghetto that the Jews are not being sent to work, but to their destruction. Well, this rumor is based on fact. But it is our wish that those who do not believe it—and you Jews are stupid optimists—should keep on not believing it, until the last minute. Therefore, you are to tell your children that we Germans are only sending them on an excursion trip. Ha, ha! Is that understood?"

54

Korczak began to think: Death, he says, is nature, and nature is murder. Now Stefa says that if eternity is eternal life, then it is eternal murder. The murderer says that nature is murder, and poor Stefa also says . . . and as for the children . . .

"Very well," he said to the Nazi. "But if we are to do this, then we will have to create in the minds of the children the illusion . . ."

"Of course! Of course! Have you any suggestions? You're an educator, aren't you?"

"The authorities will have to permit the children to sing hiking songs."

"Splendid!" Von Blutenau exclaimed. "It's a deal. You have my word. You know, you're a sharp one, you shitty Jew. You'll be working for us. If you will work for us, you will prolong your own life—for at least another year. A whole year, do you understand? You will march ahead of them, and when the sealed train pulls into the station, the children will march aboard, but you will stay behind. Splendid! Ha, ha! Splendid, Doctor Insect!"

11. THE MARCH TO THE UMSCHLAGPLATZ

The deportation of Jews from the Warsaw ghetto began during the second part of July, 1942, and stopped in October of that year. The liquidation of children's homes and orphanages began during the month of August. By that time everyone knew the truth about the "resettlement."

One early August morning, shouts came from the courtyard of the orphanage: "'Raus! 'Raus!"[9] It was a hot morning. The sun shone fiercely upon the houses in the ghetto, smothering them. The children set down their

9. "Everybody out! Out!"

coffee mugs and ran down the steps. Some time before, Korczak had had a long talk with them. He had explained to them the ideas presented in Tagore's *Post Office*. He had also told them that his children must never be afraid of anything. They were his children, and this they would always be. Whatever happened, he would remain with them. And if, some day, they would hear shouts of "*'Raus! 'Raus!* ", they were to go downstairs quickly but quietly. They were to march as if they were going on a hike as they had done before the days of the ghetto, five abreast, and they were to sing.

"Will you sing? Promise me that you will."

"We'll sing! We'll sing!" Abrasha had shouted, and all the children who had gathered to hear the doctor's talk had repeated the promise after him.

Korczak had taken out the flag, looked at it, caressed it and handed it to Abrasha. He was going to march in the lead and Abrasha would follow him with the flag. Whatever would happen, they were to know that it would not matter as long as he, the doctor, would be with them. All he asked was that they remain together, march together, look at him, look at the flag and sing hiking songs such as, for instance, this one:

> We're marching, marching, into the great outdoors,
> Marching, marching, one, two, three!
> One, two, three! We're marching two by two!
> The countryside is waiting, and so—
> We're marching, marching on!

And so the children set out on their journey.

Abrasha turned to Korczak and quoted a sentence from Tagore's play:

"There's a special quality in the air today."

Korczak's children formed a separate group, marching in close order. They were not all the same age, but all of them, including Abrasha and the doctor, were singing. Whenever the storm troopers lashed them with their whips, they drowned the pain by singing even louder. Nothing mattered, as long as the doctor was with them. No power on earth was able to stop their singing, not even when Von Blutenau hurled himself at Abrasha, tore the flag from his hand, flung it to the ground and stamped upon it. The flag seemed to him like a living thing which he wanted to trample to death.

He was drunk and in a jovial mood. He tried to pull Korczak's beard. When the storm troopers wanted to make the children stop their singing, he did not permit it.

"Don't you think this is amusing, comrades? Let them sing, those mad, dirty dogs! They *do* have special permission from the authorities, you know."

His men looked at him and joined in his laughter. They were escorting the procession on either side, left and right. They were aping the songs, making faces and winking at each other. From time to time the whup, whup of a whip was heard. The children looked at the doctor and at Abrasha, and they kept on singing.

And so they arrived at the Umschlagplatz. The train bound for Treblinka was already there, waiting. One hundred children climbed aboard one car; the other hundred entered another. In the last minute, Von Blutenau rushed up to Korczak.

"Splendid!" he guffawed. "Splendid! You, of course, will stay here with us — under our arrangement, you know—"

Korczak flung Von Blutenau's hand from his shoulder. "Don't touch me, you Nazi dog!" he shouted, and before Von Blutenau was able to recover from his surprise,

Korczak had leaped onto the sloping gangplank which
led into the sealed car. He entered the car. The train
began to move.

12. THE AWAKENING

Korczak was the first to awaken on the other side of
that which is called life.

His two hundred children, including Abrasha, were
still asleep. Stefa had arrived there before them. She was
moving about like a sleepwalker. Korczak gently touched
her shoulder. She trembled; Korczak had awakened her.

"Here we are, all of us," he said. "They'll all wake up
soon!"

She spoke as if to herself. "I see that there is no death.
But there is also no God."

Korczak laughed.

"A real Warsaw lady, that's what you are. You think
He should have come to call on you. He should have
raised His hat, bowed from the waist and said, 'I kiss
your hand, Madame,' and introduced Himself properly,
'I have the honor to be Mister God.' "

The air was pure and fresh like the sea. Here, there
was no room for the mockers and the insulters, the mes-
sengers from chaos, for the non-humans who use men to
act the part of Cain to kill his own brother, the eternal
Abel. Even breathing was not the same here. There was
a breeze, which was spirit at the same time, just like the
wind that had hovered above the waters at the time of
Creation.

Together, they made the rounds of the sleeping children, just as they would have done on earth. When they
came to Abrasha, Stefa cried out from sheer joy, so that
Abrasha awoke. Clutched in his hand was the flag, which

had been torn to shreds on earth. Now the flag, too, trembled and came back to life. Its green had taken on a new quality, and the blue Star of David shone differently against the background of white. Still holding the flag in his hand, Abrasha began to sing. The doctor and Stefa joined in. Gradually, the singing awakened the others. Their bodies were diaphanous and weightless. Slowly, they grouped themselves in circles, a wheel within a wheel; together, they resembled one huge phosphorescent globe. They were silent and eager with anticipation. None of them sang any more. The singing now was all inside their weightless, luminescent bodies, shimmering in a multitude of colors.

Majestic figures emerged from the opposite side. They took seats around an ethereal object that looked like a table. Their faces were radiant, but the radiance gave the impression of a mask that covered their real faces. They looked like ordinary men, but in fact they were superhuman or perhaps even supercelestial beings.

"Who are you?" asked Korczak—that is, Hersh, son of Joseph Goldszmit—speaking in a language he had not known he knew.

And the eldest of them replied softly, in the same language, that they were the Heavenly Court, the Court on High.

Suddenly, all the others, too, began to speak in that same language. What follows is merely a translation of what they said.

"And what is it you wish?" Korczak demanded sternly. "Will you sit in judgment over us?"

"Sit in judgment over us, indeed!" Abrasha shouted. "It is *we* who will judge *you!*" Furiously, he waved the revived flag which was raging along with him.

The figures exchanged whispers. They grew sad. The

masks of light slid from their faces. The shining thrones grew dark and moved off, along with the table.

"We understand," said the eldest of the Heavenly Court.

"We need no one except *Him*," said Doctor Goldszmit.

Stefa was still holding out. "If He is not a mere invention" she said, "then you are all in disguise. Nature is playing her game. It is nature that sent you here, and God does not exist. He is a figment of the imagination."

The figures disappeared.

The eyes of Dr. Goldszmit, formerly Korczak, followed them in silence. Then, facing the others, the doctor began to speak. He was holding Abrasha close. Behind the two stood Stefa, her ethereal body trembling violently.

Although the children could not understand the words Korczak was saying, they were able to grasp their essence. That essence was clear and infused itself into them. It was made of the same stuff as that special purity which, in circles within circles, had encompassed their weightless, astral bodies. It was not they but their bodies that grasped it.

The doctor spoke like his father, the lawyer, might have spoken in court before his illness. Even his gestures were the same.

He spoke in a language whose words were emanations of thought. These emanations were transmitted to each and every one of the others in thin, vibrating waves. Everyone joined in the vibrations.

Transmuted into human speech, this is what the doctor said:

"There was a time when I believed that God was one with nature. But nature is on the side of the murderers. If that is God, then He would be that pinhead which rises above the multitude of the mockers, and He would be the master destroyer. What concerns us is a God who is not *against* man, but for him. A God whose cruelty is merely a mask for His mercy. This is the God in whom endless generations believed and on whom my forefathers called throughout the ages. If He does not exist, then the murderer is justified. But if He does exist, then I have a thousand questions to ask Him, one more difficult than the other. For me, it would be enough to know His absolute Presence. Not His Presence within me, because then I myself would be God, a pitiful, deflated god. I mean another Presence—outside myself, above me. If I can be *certain* of His Presence then there will be an answer for my every question, even if my limited intellect would never be able to grasp it. On my own behalf, and on behalf of two hundred Jewish children who are here with me, and also on behalf of my devoted, non-believing assistant, I have the audacity— and justifiably so—to challenge such a God to a brief test. If He is not an abstraction, then He is personal. And if He is a personal, or a super-personal, personality, then He must know each one of us personally, beginning with the youngest child. He must have a personal, unique destiny in store for each and every one of us. He cannot be a mere statistician. If I, for example, am nothing more than an item in His statistics, then He does not exist, even if He is there. In the name of everyone present here, and also in the name of everyone who is not here but in another Yonder, the personal God who, I would like to believe, is more than a mere product of my wishes, is hereby challenged to answer a few simple questions:

"Will all the children here have *one and the same* impersonal destiny? Dost Thou know *them*? Dost Thou know *me*? Dost Thou know my name, who I am, and who my father was? Are we all known to Thee? I do not want to ask Thee any more questions, because man's questions about Thy ways are endless, and Thy answers to these questions would have to be accepted even if they are not understood. If Thou wilt answer only to the little I am asking now, it will be sufficient for me. From Thy answer, if it will be heard, I will know whether Thou art the true God, the God of uniqueness and of ultimate responsibility."

A long time went by before a voice sounded forth from the hidden places on high. The voice drifted down and down, as if descending a flight of steps, until at last it came to a stop and clothed itself in words from that astral language which only soul-bodies can understand. Translated into human speech, the answer was as follows:

"I know you as I know all My creatures. I know the number of the stars and I count every man's tears. Zvi Hirsh, son of Joseph, of the house of Goldszmit: I know your father; I know your mother; I know all your ancestors. I know exactly in which one of My worlds each of them is today. As for the one who is standing behind you—the cry of her thoughts has come before Me. Her unbelief has not abated. Her mind cries out: 'Thou art nothing, anyway!' But she, and you, and the two hundred children who are here with you, and all the children and all the grownups whom My enemies and the enemies of My people have already destroyed and will yet destroy—at the proper time they will return through the mystery of transmigration, each one living his own unique life and fulfilling his destiny. Justice swells in My most hidden places; no eye has ever beheld it. I have commanded it to wait, and therefore it is waiting. But Mine is the reward and Mine the vengeance. A day will come when you will be the husband of her who loes not believe in Me, though every tear from her eye and the sadness of her heart are known to Me. And he whom you call by the name of Abrasha will, through the mystery of transmigration, become the child of her womb and will be the son of both of you. He will wage My wars and the flag will belong to him. All this will come to pass at the appointed time, in a new Jerusalem."

The voice began to recede. It ascended step by step, step over step, higher and higher, and so it rose and vanished into the very last of the hidden reaches beyond words.

AARON ZEITLIN

Translated from the Yiddish
by HADASSAH ROSENSAFT
and GERTRUDE HIRSCHLER

Korczak with his children

JANUSZ KORCZAK

GHETTO DIARY

PREFACE

This is the first printing of a typewritten copy, the only one saved, of the manuscript which was handed to me under Korczak's will a few days after his deportation to Treblinka[1] together with all residents of the Children's Home.

At that time I did not consider my apartment at Zoliborz a sufficiently safe place for this valuable document, so I asked Maryna Falska[2] to hide it somewhere in Our Home at Bielany, and I managed to pass it to her before my arrest. Wladyslaw Cichosz, an employee at Our Home, following Falska's instructions bricked it up in the attic of the orphanage building.

After the war the papers were recovered and passed on to me when I returned from the concentration camps.

Korczak wrote his *Diary* in the ghetto mainly between May and August 1942, although for some time, from 1939, his growing sense of desolation had made him anxious to leave a final testament. *"Not so much an attempt at a synthesis as a grave of attempts, experiments, errors. Perhaps it may prove of use to somebody, some time, in fifty years . . ."*

He wrote the first pages in January 1940, then put the work aside. Two years later, in the face of approaching extinction, he resumed, and carried on more or less systematically to the end.

---

1. Treblinka—a town near Warsaw where at the end of 1940 a concentration camp was organized. About a million people, chiefly Jews, were put to death there.

2. Maryna Falska (1877–1944), Korczak's friend and disciple, manager of Our Home at the Warsaw suburb Bielany, an orphanage for Polish children.

In order to understand and properly evaluate them it is necessary to visualize the place, time and conditions of their being written.

Thus—the ghetto, a relatively small district of the capital, increasingly constricted by walls, packed with over half a million Jewish population from Warsaw and nearby towns. *"The district of the damned!,"* Korczak calls it, and elsewhere in the *Diary* he writes: *"The appearance of the district changes from day to day: A prison—a plague-stricken area—a lunatic asylum—a casino. Monaco. The stake—your head."*

Famine and typhus were decimating the population. People dropped dead in the streets. Pinkert's Last Service could not keep pace with the removal of corpses. Cleared in the morning, they piled up again by the evening. Normal. Children played on the sidewalks, among bodies covered with newspapers—unnoticed, meaningless as the notice on the wall:

"Always keep your body clean. Dirt breeds lice; lice, typhus!"

Time—in the sense of a normal perspective of days and months—did not exist. There was an ephemeral present instant—and eternity. Lying down to sleep, nobody was sure that he would not be wakened by the sound of a prison van—or shot dead in bed. Going out, nobody knew whether he would return or be rounded up in the street and find himself in a cattle truck. In this district resembling a sprung trap, the dread of death omnipresent, there existed only the possibility of smuggling an existence from one instant to the next, or of utter resignation—the fusion of life in some extrapersonal great existence. In something having eternal meaning and dignity: Struggle—truth and beauty—God. . . .

In the ghetto were gathered large numbers of the intelligentsia, including many creative workers. They sought to the very last to sustain human life on remainders of contemporary knowledge and culture. Scholars and artists were engrossed in their work. Young people flocked to clandestine schools and courses, lectures by professors in specialized fields. Drama studios, artistic troupes, exhibitions, concerts, meetings with authors, lectures by eminent scholars attracted large audiences.

. . . .

. . . .

In this district of superimposed contrasts, under conditions endlessly macabre, the absolutely normal—so it seems to me and I should like to call attention to it—was non-existent. No one could suffer the atmosphere of a ghetto and an Auschwitz and emerge unflawed. Everyone, victim and henchman alike, was left inevitably with some psychical taint.

When he was writing the *Diary*, Korczak was sixty-four, his constitution ruined,[3] succumbing to the burden of full responsibility for the fate of more than two hundred children and adolescents, from seven to seventeen-eighteen years of age, including a considerable number of former residents who turned to him for protection and shelter.

The institution was housed in a corner building—16

3. During this period (May 1942) Korczak suffered from weakening of the heart muscle, hernia, bladder trouble and wet pleurisy after pneumonia. His feet were swelling. "His health is in ruins," said the doctors when they refused to perform a hernia operation. "His heart will not be able to withstand it."

Sienna Street and 9 Sliska Street—the former site of the Merchants Club.[4]

During the removal of the Children's Home to the ghetto, members of the Gestapo stole a cartload of potatoes. The Old Doctor went in his uniform to the Nazi administration of the city.

The Germans, surprised that some Pole, a military man, was interested in the fate of a Jewish orphanage, started questioning him:

"But is it any of your business?"

"I'm a doctor."

"Great, so why don't you take care of Polish children, you're not a Jew, are you?"

"Yes, I'm a Jew."

"In that case why aren't you wearing an armband?"

They took him to the Pawiak prison, beat him up, and insisted he tell them who his accomplices were and what organization gave him orders to stage such a "shameless manifestation."

Former pupils managed to gather sufficient funds to buy him out of prison before he was sentenced. He returned to the children—with the Children's Home already in the ghetto.

The life of the Children's Home was in fact concentrated in the big hall on the second floor, with a few small back rooms tacked on. By night, it served as dormitory, by day for meals and classes. Ingeniously arranged chests and cabinets partitioned it into classrooms, linen storeroom, reading room, and other special-purpose accommodations. All Children's Home events and per-

4. It had been moved here from 92 Krochmalna Street, which was outside the ghetto walls.

formances were held on the third floor in the onetime ballroom. There, for example, Tagore's *The Post Office* was staged.

Peace, order, good management prevailed in the house as if the children had lived there a long time. The Korczakian child community organization—court of peers, self-government, school newspaper, fixed schedule of daily routines and occupations such as monitoring duties, school hours—all were maintained. The children studied, cleaned and tidied the house, worked in the linen room, the kitchen. Regularly, every week they were weighed and measured. Only the oldest boys went to work on building sites within the ghetto or at the Eastern Railway Station, unloading coal or laying rails. This gave them the chance to barter this or that, and bring back some food.

Food at the Children's Home was poor—but by ghetto standards luxurious. In the morning, a slice of bread, a cup of black coffee substitute or hot water mixed with colored saccharin and called "tea." For dinner— potatoes, or groats mixed with horse blood, nourishing and so well seasoned as to be quite tasty. Occasionally, horse meat and cod liver oil appeared on the table. On holidays, even some sort of darkish rye cookies were baked.

Stefania Wilczynska was in charge of the daily routine at the Children's Home. Korczak would go out in the morning and return late. He regularly went to the institution for destitute children at 39 Dzielna Street, that "children's slaughter and charnelhouse." He took it upon himself to rehabilitate that institution and fought a hopeless, losing battle against the unscrupulous, thieving staff. He would make calls at the Jewish Community Office, Jüdisches Hilfskomitee, the homes of the rich, even the offices of notorious, utterly compromised col-

71

laborators. He begged, threatened, quarreled. He cared not who it was who gave and whether enough remained for others. He was the father of two hundred children and must provide for them.

This was a different Korczak. Exhausted, irritable, suspicious, ready to raise hell over a barrel of sauerkraut, a sack of flour. Bear this in mind, too, when reading the *Diary*, especially Korczak's opinions on certain people, on his differences with them.

From such rounds he returns in the evening completely worn out, with figures in his notebook representing his day's booty, and behind his eyes the image of the ghetto. At night, he thinks and writes. He writes in the sickroom where lie several of the weakest children and a dying man, father of one of the pupils, approaching the end of a long, serious illness.

It seems unbelievable that he could still write.

In such surroundings, in that state of health, after such a day, he no longer has the strength or will to write for publication: he can only talk to himself on paper, making notes in haphazard abbreviations, almost a cipher; something of his chance thoughts, some memories, a fleeting impression. . . . The *Diary* has become no more than a register of psychological moments. This is neither the legendary Korczak nor the real Korczak. This is a man fragmented into moments, impulses, fibers—a third being, uncoordinated; the writing is more mysterious in its trembling close-up, in its burning sincerity. It long continues to torment with its suffering—and it is astonishing how a great testament and work of art brings home to one the calamities of the human condition, makes one more human.

The very first pages of the *Diary* reveal the intention to rule off the account, to transfer to somebody in the distant future the last testament of his own experiences, dissensions and beliefs. The introductory reflections are examples of the literary craft—sentences beautifully molded, perfect, ready for the printer. But the further he proceeds with the work the more does his initial conception become confused and shattered. Complete psychological detachment from the agony of the ghetto simply proves to be impossible.

Strikingly varied is the form, from stylistically elaborated sections—for instance, the introductory reflections on the subject of old age—through the concise chronicle accounts right up to thoughts coded in abbreviations, jotted down for his own use to be developed later if time and life permitted. The same applies to the contents. The retrospective breaths of self-analysis are crossed by the images of macabre reality, from which vision repeatedly embraces the future, indifferent to the now worthless personal life, striving still to probe the ultimate fate of the world and man.

Even so, Korczak remains himself from the very first to the very last page. Frank—brutally so at times—in every single clause, with his evangelist's heart and keen eye for the grotesque. Faithful to the truths professed over a lifetime—he continues to defend them with the same fire of the controversialist and the practice of shocking the bourgeois conventions specific to the "Young Poland"[5] literary trend, exaggerating his visions of eugenics and euthanasia, balancing upon a razor's edge between abolute reason and absurdity.

And to the very end he preserved that passion for cognition, what his self-analysis termed the *"searching mind"* for which *"not the mechanism but the actual sub-*

5. A trend of artistic and literary character, developed chiefly in Cracow at the turn of 19th to 20th centuries. It was directed against the rationalistic point of view. The chief objective was to come back to romantic traditions.

stance of the thing" alone becomes compelling and worthy of probing.

In the deluge of total bestiality, he seeks frantically for some minimal scrap of sense, tries to take an impassioned view of the other side, of the alien point of view with its inhuman philosophy, and prepares *"History's program speech,"* a theme which, unless his specific approach and personality are comprehended, may create the weird impression of some apology of Hitlerism.

In July 1942, when it was becoming obvious that the ghetto was marked for liquidation, Maryna Falska made a last attempt to save Korczak. I repeat . . . a last attempt . . . because earlier his friends outside the walls had frequently urged him to leave the ghetto and find asylum with them. This time, everything was scrupulously organized—a German identity card in an assumed name, a safe room prepared by Falska near Our Home on the periphery of Warsaw. I went to the ghetto on a pass for a water and sewage system inspector who, on his way back, was to take with him a locksmith working on the ghetto territory.

It is difficult to describe the psychological shock experienced by any normal man in this sinister quarter of people under sentence of death, the sense of personal humiliation and shame at being a so-called Aryan. Only in the Children's Home was it possible to recover, to regain self-control. There it was like an oasis. Everything running according to the normal, long established routine, everything exuding order, calm, good management. Yet the children were quieter, slower in their movements, and "Pandoktor" looked ill, wasted, stooping. At sixty-four, his health was wrecked: at the expense of stupendous daily effort he was finding food, medicines and clothes, was tottering under this terrible responsibility and care for the fate of two hundred children and youngsters.

I explained that now there was only a single chance to save a few from perishing, that there could be no postponement. If the Doctor would break up the boarding school, some of the children and teachers would perhaps have a chance to escape beyond the walls. Let him order that, and come away at once with me.

He looked at me as though disappointed in me, as though I had proposed a betrayal or an embezzlement. I wilted under his gaze and he turned away, saying quietly but not without reproach in his voice:

"You know, of course, why Zalewski was beaten up. . . ."

Piotr Zalewski, a former grenadier in the Tsarist army, has been janitor and in charge of central heating in the Children's Home for twenty years. When the order for removal came, Zalewski wanted to go to the ghetto, too. Wolanska, who for many years had run the laundry in the Home, went with a similar application to the Nazi police. Her they merely kicked out, but to Zalewski they administered a bestial reminder that he was an Aryan. (During the Warsaw Uprising in 1944, Zalewski met his death in the courtyard of the Children's Home.)

So Korczak recalled Zalewski with an obvious though unformulated reproach—you see, a janitor would not leave the children because he was attached to them, and you propose that I, their tutor, their father. . . . Is it thinkable that I should leave the children alone to suffocate in a gas chamber? How could I live after that? He could not. He did not.

By way of farewell, and as a sort of absolution, he said he would send me his *Diary*, which he was writing day by day in the Ghetto.

On the 5th of August, 1942, began the march of the

children and teachers of the Children's Home, led by Janusz Korczak and Stefania Wilczynska. Neatly clad in their best clothes they marched in fours, steadily, under their flag—the gold four-leaf clover on a field of green, as dreamed by King Matthew, because green is the symbol of everything that grows—fluttering above their heads. They marched through the hushed streets of Warsaw to the Umschlagplatz, near the Gdansk Railway Station. Here they were all loaded into chlorinated freight cars. The train set out for the Treblinka extermination camp.

He kept his word—as always. Shortly after the 5th of August, I received the *Diary*.

Needless to say, the publishers would not presume to correct Korczak in certain formal blemishes resulting from the conditions under which his *Diary* was written, and certainly any dabbling with content, the very substance of the subject matter, would be unthinkable. However some of the opinions expressed by this great writer and civic leader may appear to readers—they must not be muted, far less concealed. The *Diary* is printed in full without any editorial adjustment, with such reverence as is due this document of the last days and thoughts of a man of this stature.

IGOR NEWERLY

PART ONE

Reminiscences make a sad, depressing literature.

Artists, scholars, politicians and great leaders of men—all of them start out with ambitious plans, resolute actions, aggressive, bold moves. They climb higher and higher, overcome obstacles, extend the range of their influence and, armed with experience and a large number of friends, they press—with increasing ease and success—stage by stage, toward their objective. This takes ten years, sometimes twice, three times that long. And then . . .

Then comes fatigue: bit by bit, still doggedly moving in the once chosen direction—only now along a more leisurely road, with diminished zeal and with a painful realization that their life is not what they had meant it to be, that it is not enough, and especially difficult to face single-handed—they find that the only thing they had achieved is more graying hair, wrinkles on the once smooth and bold forehead, failing eyesight, slower circulation and tired feet.

What has happened? It is old age.

Some will resist, try not to give in, to go on as usual, even at a faster pace and more aggressively, for time is short. They deceive themselves, they fight back, rebel and thrash about. Others, in sad resignation, not only give up but even regress.

"I can't go on. I won't even try. What for? I can no longer understand the world. Ah, to recover the years gone by, reduced to ashes, the strength squandered in blundering, the wasteful momentum of the old zeal . . ."

New people appear, a new generation, new needs.

Now they begin to irritate him, as he irritates them; first there are some misunderstandings, later—lasting lack of understanding. Their gestures, their walk, their eyes, their white teeth and smooth faces, even though their lips are silent . . .

Everything and everyone around you, the entire world, and you yourself, and your stars, keep saying:

"This is it . . . Your sun has set . . . Now it is our turn . . ." Your time is over . . . You say we don't know very much . . . We shall not argue with you—you do know more than we do, you're experienced, but you must let us try our own way . . .

Such is the order of life.

So it is with man and animal, so it seems to be with trees, and who knows, perhaps with stones as well.

Today is their will, their power, their time. Yours— today old-age, and the day after tomorrow— decrepitude.

The hands of the clocks move faster and faster.

The stony gaze of the sphinx asks the eternal question:

"Who is it that walks on all fours in the morning, briskly on two legs at noon, and on three in the evening?"

It is you—leaning on your cane, gazing into the dying cold rays of the setting sun. . . .

I shall try to do something different with the story of my own life. Perhaps the idea is good, perhaps it will work, perhaps this is the right way.

When you dig a well, you do not start at the deepest end. First you break up the upper layer, throw the earth aside, shovelful after shovelful, not knowing what is underneath, how many tangled roots, what other obstacles, how many stones forgotten and buried by yourself and by others.

80

The decision is made. There's strength enough to start. And, in fact, is any work ever really finished? Roll up your sleeves. A firm grip on the shovel. Let's go!

One, two; one, two . . .

"God help you, old man! But what's your plan?"

"Can't you see for yourself? I seek subterranean springs; I push aside clear, cool streams of water and browse through the memories."

"May I help you?"

"No, my dear friend, this each man must do alone. Nobody can undertake the job for him or replace him. Everything else we can do together so long as you trust and respect me; but this final work of mine—I must do myself."

"May God help you!"

Now then . . .

I intend to refute a deceitful book by a false prophet. This book has done a great deal of harm.

Also sprach Zarathustra.

And I spoke, I had the honor to speak, with Zarathustra. His wise mysteries, profound, difficult and piercing, have landed you, you poor philosopher, behind the dark walls and the heavy bars of a lunatic asylum, for that is how it was. It says so in black and white:

"Nietzsche died insane, at odds with life!"

In my book I want to prove that he had died painfully at odds with truth.

The very same Zarathustra had taught me something different. But perhaps I had better hearing, perhaps I listened with greater care.

In this much we are together: the road of the master and my own road, the disciple's, were both difficult. There were more defeats than successes, many devia-

81

tions and thus much time and effort wasted, or seemingly wasted.

For in the hour of reckoning I am not inside a solitary cell of the saddest hospital in the world but surrounded by butterflies and grasshoppers, and glowworms, and I hear a concert of crickets and a soloist high up in the sky—the skylark.

Merciful Lord!

Thank you, Merciful Lord, for the meadow and the bright sunsets, for the refreshing evening breeze after a hot day of toil and struggle.

Thank you, Merciful Lord, for having arranged so wisely to provide flowers with fragrance, glowworms with the glow, and make the stars in the sky sparkle.

How joyous old age is.

How delectable the silence.

How sweet the repose.

"Man is so immeasurably blessed with Thy gifts, whom Thou hast created and saved . . ."

Well then. Here I do.

One, two . . .

Two old men sit warming themselves in the sun.

"Tell me, you old codger, how is it that you are still alive?"

"Well, I've led a respectable, sensible life free of shocks and sudden turns. I don't smoke, drink, play cards, chase women. Was never hungry, never too tired, lived without haste and took no risks. With precision and moderation. I did not strain my heart or exhaust my lungs or overtax my brain. Moderation, peace and reflection. That is why I am still alive."

"And how about you, friend?"

"Somewhat differently. Wherever a bruise or a bump on the head was to be found, there I was. As only a young pup, I had my first taste of revolution and shoot-ing. Sleepless nights and enough time in the cooler as would take the rough edges off any youngster. Then the war. I took it as it came. It had to be sought out in remote places, beyond the Ural mountains, beyond Lake Baikal, across the Tatar, Kirghiz, Buryat country, right up to China. I rested for a time in the Manchurian Vil-lage of Taoway-jou and—another revolution. Then came peace, of a sort, for a brief while. I drank vodka, to be sure, and more than once staked my life—not just a crumpled bank note—on a single card. But I had no time for girls, although, were it not for the fact they're such a greedy lot and occupy so many of your nights, and be-sides they do get pregnant . . . A nasty habit. It hap-pened to me once. Left a bad taste in my mouth for life. I had enough of it, the threats and the tears. I smoked cigarettes endlessly. During the day, during any discus-sion, one after another, like a chimney. And there isn't a bit of me left in sound health. Adhesions, aches, rap-tures, scars. I am falling to pieces, I groan, I am un-stitched, but I'm alive. And how I live! Anyone who has gotten in my way will tell you. I can still kick pretty hard, that you can believe. Even now it happens that a whole gang will slink away when they see me. And I do have followers and friends as well . . ."

"So have I. And children and grandchildren. And you, my friend?"

"Two hundred"

"You like to joke, don't you . . ."

*

It is now the year 1942. The month of May. The month of May is cold this year. And tonight is the quietest of all nights. It is five in the morning. The little ones are asleep. There are really two hundred of them. In the east wing—Miss Stefa, and I in the west, in the so-called "solitary."

My bed stands in the middle of the room. Under the bed—a bottle of vodka; on the night table, black bread and a jug of water.

Good old Felek, he has sharpened the pencils at both ends. I could write with a fountain pen; one was given to me by Hadaska, the other by the father of a difficult boy.

I already have a groove impressed in my finger by the pencil. It just now occurs to me that I could do it differently, more conveniently, that a pen is easier.

It was not for nothing that as a child my dad called me a gawk and a clod and, when he flew into rage, even an idiot and an ass. Grannie was the only one who believed in my star. Otherwise all I heard was—lazy, crybaby, idiot (as I've said before), and good-for-nothing.

But more about that later.

They were right. Both equally right. Half grannie, half dad.

But more about that later.

Lazy . . . quite right, I don't like writing. Thinking—yes, definitely. No difficulty. It's like telling myself fairy tales.

Once I read somewhere: "There are people who do not think, in the way that some say 'I don't smoke'."

I do think.

One, two, one, two. I gawk compulsively at each clumsy shovelful from my well. I ponder over it for some ten minutes. And not just because today I'm weak in my old age.

It was always so.

Grannie would give me raisins and say: "You, philosopher."

Allegedly even then, in an intimate chat, I confided to

grannie my bold scheme to remake the world. It was—no less, no more—to throw away all money. How and where, and what to do next I probably had no idea. Do not judge me too harshly. I was only five then, and the problem was perplexingly difficult: what to do so there wouldn't be any dirty, ragged and hungry children with whom one was not allowed to play in the backyard (where under a chestnut tree, in a candy box, wrapped in cotton, was buried my first dearly beloved creature, then still only a canary)? Its death had brought about the mysterious question of religion.

I had wanted to put a cross on top of the grave. The housemaid said no, because it was only a bird, something much, much lower than man. Even to cry over it was a sin.

So much for the housemaid. What was worse, the janitor's son decided that the canary was Jewish.

And so was I.

I too was a Jew, and he—a Pole, a Catholic. It was certain paradise for him, but as for me, if I did not use dirty words and never failed dutifully to steal sugar for him from the house—I would end up, when I died, in a place which, though not hell, was nevertheless dark. And I was scared of a dark room.

Death—Jew—hell. A black Jewish paradise. Certainly plenty to think about.

*

I am in bed. The bed is in the middle of the room. My subtenants are: Monius, the younger (we have four of them), then Albert and Jerzyk. On the other side, against the wall, Felunia, Gienia and Haneczka.

The door to the boys' dormitory is open. There are

85

sixty of them. A bit farther east are sixty girls, peacefully asleep.

The rest are on the top floor. It is May, and although it has been cold the older boys can, in a pinch, sleep in the top-floor hall.

It is night. I have my notes about the night and about the sleeping children. Thirty-four small pads filled with notes. That is why it took me so long to make up my mind to write my memoirs.

I plan to write:

1. A thick volume about the night in an orphanage and about sleeping children in general.

2. A two-volume novel. It takes place in Palestine. The first night of a newly-married Halutz couple at the foot of Mount Gilboa, in a spot where a spring bubbles up; a reference to that mountain and that spring is made in the Book of Moses.

(That well of mine will be a deep one, if I have the time.)

3, 4, 5, 6. Some years ago I wrote a piece for children on the life of Pasteur. And now a continuation of that series: Pestalozzi, da Vinci, Kropotkin, Pilsudski, and a few dozen more, including Fabre, Multatuli, Ruskin and Gregor Mendel, Nalkowski, Szczepanowski, Dygasinski, Dawid.[1]

Ever heard of Nalkowski?

The world knows nothing of many great Poles.

7. Years ago I wrote a novel about King Matthew.

---

1. Jean-Henri Fabre, French entomologist (1823–1915); Multatuli, pen name of E. D. Dekker, Dutch writer (1820–1887); John Ruskin, English author and critic (1819–1900); Gregor-Johann Mendel, famous Austrian geneticist (1822–1884); Waclaw Nalkowski, eminent Polish geographer, pedagogue and civic leader (1856–1911); Stanislaw Szczepanowski, business promoter, journalist, pioneer of Polish oil industry (1846–1900); Adolf Dygasinski, Polish novelist, storyteller, journalist and pedagogue (1839–1902); Jan Wladyslaw Dawid, Polish psychologist and pedagogue (1858–1914).

Now came the time for the king-child: King David the Second.

8. Why waste the material of five hundred of the children's weight and height charts and not describe the wonderful, true, joyous work of the growth of man? In the coming five thousand years, somewhere in the abyss of time, there will be socialism; now there is anarchy. A war of poets and musicians in the most splendid of Olympic Games. A war for the most beautiful prayer, for a world hymn to God once a year.

I have forgotten to mention that now, too, a war is going on.

10. An autobiography.

Yes. About myself, about my little and important self.

Someone once said bitterly that the earth is a speck of mud suspended in space; and man is an animal who has made a career.

This may be so. But here's an addendum: this drop of mud knows what suffering is, it can love and weep and is full of longing.

And as for man's career, if you consider it carefully, the issue is highly doubtful.

It is half past six.

In the dormitory someone shouts:

"Boys, time for a bath, get up!"

I put away my pen. Should I or should I not get up? It is a long time since I have had a bath. Yesterday I caught on myself and killed without turning a hair—with one dexterous squeeze of the nail—a louse.

If I have the time, I shall write a eulogy to a louse. For our attitude toward this fine insect is unjust and unfitting.

An embittered Russian peasant once declared:

"A louse is not like a man, it will not suck up every last drop of blood."

I have written a short tale about sparrows whom I have been feeding for twenty years. I had set for myself the task of exonerating the little thieves. But who will explore the persecution of the louse?

Who if not I?

Who will come forward, who will have the courage to come forward in its defense?

*

"For the callous attempt to shift the responsibility for an orphan onto the shoulders of the community, for the arrogance of the insults, abuses and threats hurled around in a frenzy at the failure of your attempt—you, madam, have to pay within five days 500 zlotys to the "Orphans' Aid" fund.

"Taking into account the low level of your social environment, the house where you live, the fine is set rather low. I expect deceitful excuses that you did not know who it was who conducted the interview; when your youngest progeny, sent to escort me, had seen my identity card shown to the policeman, she shouted in parting: 'animal!'. I did not insist on the young person's arrest, taking into consideration her age and the fact that she was not wearing an armband.[2]

"Finally, allow me to mention that this was my second unhappy encounter with the riff-raff of the elegant house at 14 Walicow Street, for during the siege of Warsaw they refused me help carry a dying soldier, his chest wide open, into the courtyard, so that he might not die like a dog in the gutter."

2. Armband indicating that the child was Jewish.

Here are a few comments:

The lady occupants of the premises from which I was chased away with shouts of: "Get out of here, you old bastard, break your leg and your arm!"—those lady occupants were "friends" of none other than Stefania Sempolowska.[3]

I should like to enlarge of this theme, since the matter has broader implications.

Sempolowska was a fanatical advocate of the Jews, defending us against false as well as justified charges made against us by equally fanatical enemies.

The three Jewesses from Walicow Street—they were the types who by glib talk and, yes, even baptism, would force their way shamelessly into Polish society, into Polish homes and families, there to represent the Jews.

I tried repeatedly, though without effect, to explain to Miss Stefania, the enthusiast, that there could not be, nor ought there be any unison or even as much as casual contact between the Jewish scum and the Polish intellectual, moral elite.

During the thirty years of our association, this precisely was the cause of our deplorable differences and estrangements.

Wojciechowski – Pilsudski – Norwid – Mickiewicz – Kosciuszko – Zajaczek[4], who knows, perhaps Lukasiewicz[5] as well, or even Creon and Antigone—was their remoteness from one another caused precisely by their closeness?

And earlier, Nalkowski and Straszewicz, seemingly enemies, were in fact filled with longing for each other.

3. A well-known author and liberal social worker (1870–1943).

4. Some well-known Poles whom Korczak knew personally, and some historical figures.

5. Jan Lukasiewicz (1878–1956), philosopher, logician, professor at Lwow, Warsaw and Lublin universities.

How easy it is for two rogues to get together for joint enterprise in treachery, crime, fraud, but how utterly impossible a harmonious collaboration between two people who love equally well, but with a different understanding of that love, based on a different stock of experience.

I have always hated and detested Jewish peddlers of ideas and platitudes. And I have also witnessed the dignity of those Jews who, having escaped, were in hiding so as not to meet their friends from outside the trenches.

Who could forget dear old "Wojtek," a militant nationalist who, over a cup of coffee, asked almost with despair:

"Tell me, what is one to do? The Jews are digging our grave."

Or Godlewski:

"We are a weak lot. For a glass of vodka, we sell ourselves into Jewish bondage."

Or Moszczenska:

"Your virtues are a death sentence to us."

The corner of Zelazna and Chlodna. A meat shop. Overflowing a chair, an enormously fat Jewess is trying on a pair of shoes. The visiting shoemaker is kneeling in front of her. A sensitive, spiritual face. Gray hair, wise, kind eyes, serious, deep voice, on his face an expression of hopeless resignation.

"But I did warn you that these shoes . . ."

"And I am warning you that you might as well keep these shoes for your wife, mister. Are you a shoemaker, or aren't you, eh? How does it look, that foot of mine?"

And she dangles her fat foot in front of his nose, almost touching it.

"Are you blind? Can't you see how it crinkles?"

One of the worst scenes I have ever witnessed, but not the only one.

"Our people are no better."
"I know."
Well then, what's the answer?

*

Radios belong to those who have bought them. So do cars. And theater tickets. And trips, and books, and paintings.

Perhaps I might describe a group of Polish tourists I met in Athens. Taking snapshots of one another in front of, no more, no less, but the Pantheon. Chirping, giggly—but then, every pup turns in circles to catch its own tail.

Why am I writing all this?

Well, yes. The devil does exist. But even among devils some are more and some are less wicked.

*

Little Janusz and Irka built a garden in the sand, and a little house, and flowers, and a picket fence. They carried water in a matchbox. They took turns. Then they conferred: and built another house. Then they conferred: and added a chimney. They conferred: and added a well. They conferred: and added a doghouse.

The dinner bell rang. Moving toward the dining room, they turned back twice to put on the final touches, to have one more look.

All the while Musiek observed from a distance. Then he kicked down the edifice, trampled over it, hit it a long time with his stick.

When they returned after dinner, Irka said:

"I know: it's Musiek."

Born in Paris, he was offered back to his homeland and

for three years has been making life impossible for the thirty orphans in the kindergarten.

I wrote an article about him for *Special Pedagogics* advocating penal colonies; I even hinted at death penalty. He is little yet! So he'll be at large for fully fifty years!

Said dear Miss Maria with a perplexed smile:

"You must have been joking?"

"Far from it. How much human misery, how much pain, how many tears . . ."

"So you don't believe in reform?"

"I am not Adler," I said gruffly.

No one can be angry for long with Dr. Maria Grzegorzewska. The compromise: I erased the death penalty— left just the penal colony (and that only with difficulty).

Are decent people in positions of leadership condemned to Calvary for ever and ever?

Why am I writing all this?

*

Of course, it's night. Twelve thirty.

I've had a hard day.

There was the conference with two gentlemen, two high priests of social welfare. Then two interviews, one involving the row referred to earlier. Then a meeting of the Board.

Tomorrow—39 Dzielna Street.

I said to that lawyer:

"Listen, if each day things improve even by a tenth of an inch, it encourages greater effort. If things get worse each day, disaster will come and with it some change. But we are motionless."

Pay attention. What I have to say may come in handy.

There are four ways of dealing with undesirable new-comers:

1. To bribe them. To admit them to your gang and then bamboozle them.

2. To agree to anything and, watching for the moment they are off guard, to go on as usual, doing as you please. I am just one against all the rest. I assess them, at a liberal estimate, about three hours daily. They think around the clock of how to deceive me. I shall explain this when writing about thinking in one's sleep. All this is well known, anyway.

3. To wait, to mark time, lie low and when the right time comes—to discredit them.

"You see! It was his idea!"

One could lie. (They offered to leave the money in my care.)

4. To wear them out. Either they will go away or stop spying. Because why bother?

I've run out of ink.

*

I feel old whenever I reminisce about the past, the bygone years and events. I want to be young, so I make plans for the future.

What shall I do after the war?

Perhaps I will be invited to participate in building a new order in the world, or in Poland. This is highly improbable and I would not want it. I would have to keep an office, meaning the slavery of fixed working hours and contacts with people, a desk somewhere, a telephone, an armchair. Wasting time on current, petty everyday problems and contending with petty people with their petty ambitions, their influential friends, hierarchies and goals.

In sum—a yoke.

I prefer to be on my own.

When I was laid up with the typhus, I had the following vision:

A huge theater or concert hall. Crowds of people, all dressed up.

I am giving an address about war and hunger, orphans and misery.

I speak in Polish. An interpreter translates quickly into English. (All this takes place in America.) Suddenly my voice breaks. There is silence. Somewhere in the hall a cry may be heard. Running toward me is Regina. She stops in front of the dais, throws a watch on the platform and cries out: "For you—everything!" And then there is a shower of bank notes, gold and jewelry. People are tossing their rings, bracelets, necklaces. Boys from the Children's Home come running onto the stage: the Gelblat brothers, Falka, Meir Kulawski, Gluzman, Szejwacz—and they stuff all this into mattresses. The audience, deeply moved, cheer, applaud and weep.

I have no particular faith in prophecies, and yet for well over twenty years I have been waiting for the vision to come true.

I shall have something to say about Regina when I write of the strange fate of the inmates of the white house on Krochmalna Street in Warsaw.[6]

So I shall come into unlimited material means and shall open a contest for the construction of a huge orphanage in the hills of Lebanon, near Kfar Giladi.[7]

It will have large barracks-like dining rooms and dormitories. There will be small "hermit huts." For myself, on the terrace of a flat roof I will have one room, not too

6. Korczak's institution before the ghetto was at 92 Krochmalna Street.
7. A kibbutz in Northern Galilee which Korczak visited during a trip to what is now Israel.

large, with transparent walls, so that I might not miss a single sunrise or sunset and so that, writing at night, I might be able to look now and again at the stars.

Young Palestine is making arduous and honest efforts to come to terms with the earth. But the heaven's turn will also come. Otherwise all would be a misunderstanding, a mistake.

Why not Birobidjan, Uganda, California, Ethiopia, Tibet, Madagascar, India, Southern Russia or Polesie? Even England, well meaning and world-wise, does not know where to plant that handful of Jewry, small as it is.

Every year I should visit for a few weeks my native town, my friends, to talk over important, eternal problems . . .

To be sure, my dream is never monotonously the same. Each time I make certain modifications.

My most serious problem is with the construction of huts for the hermits. Those who have earned a life of solitude aspire to happiness through solitude, they can read it and must translate it into comprehensible language—*orbi et urbi*. They simply must, must, must have it; but what is it they should have? There's the rub.

Once again Moszek has forgotten to put enough carbide in the lamp. The flame is dying.

I must stop now.

Five o'clock in the morning

Good old Albert, he has let the daylight in.

The window panes are covered with black paper shades so that our lights would not interfere with the military authorities' lamp signaling, and they also say they may guide enemy planes. As if there were not enough other signals and landmarks. But folks will believe anything.

So it is light again.

People are naive and good-hearted. And probably un-happy. They have not much of an idea what happiness consists of. Everyone understands it differently.

To some, it's a delicious cholent or sausage with sauer-kraut. To others—peace, comfort, luxury. To still others—women, many and varied, or else—music, or cards, or traveling.

And everyone combats boredom and nostalgia in a different way.

Boredom—a hunger of the spirit.

Nostalgia—a thirst, a thirst for water and for flight, for freedom. And a yearning for a man, a confidant, a confes-sor, an advisor, a yearning for counsel, confession, for an understanding ear to hear my lament.

The spirit feels a longing inside the narrow cage of the body. Man feels and ponders death as though it were the end, when in fact death is merely the continuation of life, it is another life.

You may not believe in the existence of the soul, yet you must acknowledge that your body will live on as green grass, as a cloud. For you are, after all, water and dust.

"The world is the metamorphosis of evil, everlasting"—Tetmajer[8] has said.

This unbeliever, pessimist, nihilist, he too speaks of eternity.

The amoeba is immortal, and man is a colony of sixty trillion amoebas—said Maeterlinck. And he knew the experts. Because, for a dozen odd years I have tried unsuccessfully to find out how many times to multiply two billion—the population of the world.

8. Polish poet, novelist, playwright, representative of "Young Poland" (1865–1940).

My fellow teacher, Professor Paszkiewicz, said the figure was astronomical. Until by chance I found the answer in Maeterlinck's *Termites*.

There are two billion people in the world, and I constitute a community many million times greater, therefore I have the right, I have the duty to look after my own trillions toward which I have certain responsibilities.

Perhaps it is not safe to tell the general public about this, although everyone must sense it anyway, even if not altogether consciously. Anyhow, is my own universe and its fate not related to the fate of my entire generation, from the Australian cannibal islands to the workshop of a poet, a scientist looking through his telescope set on a snowbound peak or a polar plain?

When little Genka coughs during the night, in an altruistic sense I feel pity for her, but egoistically I weigh the disturbance in the night, the concern for her health against: maybe she's contagious? the expense of the extra food, the trouble and the costs involved in sending her to the country.

I feel sleepy. Before my beehive begins to buzz, I shall try to nap for an hour.

I am convinced that in a future rational society the dictatorship of the clock will come to an end. To sleep and eat when you feel like it.

How lucky that the doctors and the police cannot prescribe how many times I may be allowed to breathe per minute, how many times my heart has the right to beat.

I do not like to sleep at night because then I cannot sleep in the daytime. Bread and water taste better at night.

It is nonsense to put a child to bed for ten hours of uninterrupted sleep.

The man of the future will be astonished to find that

we used cut flowers to decorate our apartments. And hung paintings on our walls. And used animal skins for carpets.

They are scalps, scalps of flowers and scalps of our noble younger brothers, the animals.

And the canvas, smeared with colors, which one does not even see after a time, with dust settling on the frame and vermin on the back . . .

How petty, savage and miserable was that primitive man of thousands of years ago!

And they will lament over our primitive systems of education.

What stifling ignorance of the lifeless language!

When associating with "the simple folk," now and then I would fish out talent among the children.

Somewhere in Solec, in a laborer's shack, I came across some sketches drawn by a small boy: a horse was a horse, a tree was a tree, a ship was a ship.

I took a roll of the drawings, those that seemed to me to be the best, to show to a well-known painter.

He examined them and said with a grimace:

"It's absolutely worthless. Copies. Only this one, perhaps, is passable."

And then he said something odd:

"Everyone should know how to sketch in pencil what he wants to retain in memory. Not to be able to do that is to be illiterate."

How often did I recollect this irrefutable truth.

Here is a scene, a face, a tree, but in a moment they will be lost to me forever. What a shame, what a pity!

The tourists have found a way: the photograph. And now even film. A generation of children and young people is growing up today who will be able to watch their own first clumsy steps.

The unforgettable sight of the dormitory coming

awake: A sleepy gaze, languid motions, or a sudden leaping out of bed. One of them rubs his eyes, another wipes the corners of his mouth with the sleeve of his nightshirt, still another strokes his ear, stretches, or holding an article of clothing in his hand stares motionless into space.

Energetically or phlegmatically, skillfully or clumsily, with self-assurance or timidly, with precision or carelessly, deliberately or mechanically.

These are real tests: you can sum him up at a glance, who he is and why he always acts this way, or if not, why today.

A lecturer provides commentary to a film:

"Look carefully, please (he points with a cane, as though to a map). A resentful exchange of glances between the two on the right shows their mutual dislike; their beds should not be adjacent.

"The squinting eyes of this one prove conclusively that he is nearsighted.

"Do not trust the endurance of this boy over here: he shows strain, nervousness of movements, a variable rhythm, interruptions in his seemingly steady haste. Perhaps he has taken on a wager, has challenged to a race that boy on the left, the one at whom he keeps glancing.

"And for this one I predict a bad day today. Something is wrong with him. While washing, making his bed, at breakfast, very soon, or in an hour, he will get into an argument or a fight, or will talk back to the teacher."

We were standing, the two of us, by the window while a new game of "two fires" was about to be organized.

A noble, chivalrous game.

A ten-year-old expert was my instructor:

"He'll get a beating right off, because he's tired. And that one'll show what he can do halfway through the game, as soon as he tries harder. This one will be thrown out. See that one, he's got eyes in the back of his head, looks to the right and passes to the left. This one will surrender, sneakily, to cut out those other two later on. And that one will get mad, quarrel and cry."

Should the forecast prove wrong, the expert knows exactly why and explains. In his calculations and assessment of the situation, he has failed to take this or that into account:

"He's playing this way because yesterday he broke a window and now he's scared. That one's got the sun in his eyes and that other one hasn't gotten used to the ball, it's too hard for him. A sore foot—that one. This wonderful shot's his friend's doing—always backs him up!"

He reads the game like a musician reads the score, commenting on the moves as if it were a game of chess.

If I have a vague idea about it all, I owe it to my devoted instructors. How patient, selfless, friendly they are; what a slow, inept student I am.

No wonder: I was over forty when soccer appeared in this country, while these boys crawled on all fours holding a ball under the arm.

Five thick volumes:
1. Plain ball.
2. Soccer.
3. "Two fires."
4. The psychology and philosophy of ball playing.
5. Life stories, interviews. Descriptions of outstanding shots, games, stadiums.

And a hundred kilometers of film.

If I have anticipated a reaction well in advance then nothing irritates me, makes me impatient or angry.

Today the class will be restless because it's April Fool's Day, because it's hot, because in three days there's to be an outing, because the holidays are in a week, because I've got a headache.

I remember a school teacher, already experienced in the profession, who would get indignant at the boys because their hair grew so fast. And I remember a young boarding-school worker, a beginner, who used to start her routine report on the girls' bedtime with:

"Tonight the girls were impossible. At nine they were still talking. At ten, still whispering and laughing. And all this because the principal had me on the carpet, because I was angry, because I was in a hurry, because tomorrow I have an exam, because I mislaid my stockings, because I've received a disturbing letter from home."

Someone will say:

"What is a film worth if the children know they are being filmed?"

Easy:

The camera is fixed in one place. The operator turns the handle with no film in the camera, at different times and angles. The children are promised they will see the film when it's ready, but every time something seems to go wrong. Sequences are repeatedly taken of troublesome, difficult, unpopular children and uninteresting happenings. The children are never once told to be natural, to look this way and not that way or to "act normally." The floodlights are switched on and off at random. Then again a game is interrupted and a grueling rehearsal ordered.

After a period of initial fascination comes impatience. Finally, they cease to take any notice. After a week, a month. But why bother explaining it? Certainly it is done like that. There's no other way.

A teacher who does not know this is an illiterate, a fool if he does not understand it.

In the future, every teacher will have to be a stenographer and a cameraman.

And dictaphones, and the radio?

And the epoch-making experiments of Pavlov?

Or the horticulturist who by crossbreeding and grafting has grown roses without thorns and "pears on willow trees"?[9]

We do already have a basic sketch of a man—perhaps even a photograph? Perhaps we're not far off? All that's needed is skillful and conscientious retouching.

Others are afraid to sleep in the daytime in order not to spoil the night. It's the reverse with me. I sleep at night unwillingly—I prefer the daytime.

May 15, six o'clock

I already know about the girls half of what I ought to know.

It went something like this. A question:

"You know, Helcia, you're a restless person."

She:

"I am a person?"

"Why, of course. You're not a puppy."

She pondered. After a long pause, surprised:

"I am a person. I am Helcia. I am a girl. I am Polish. I am mummy's little daughter. I am a Warsaw inhabitant . . . What a lot of things I am!"

And again:

"I have a mummy, a daddy, a grannie, two grannies, a granddaddy, a dress, hands, a doll, a little table, a canary, an apron. And do I have you?"

A certain nationalist told me:

"A Jew, a sincere patriot, is at best a 'Warsawer' or 'Cracower', but not a Pole."

9. A Polish saying corresponding to achieving the impossible. (Transl.)

I was rather taken aback.

I did admit frankly that I am unmoved by Lwow, Poznan, Gdynia, the Augustow Lakes or Zaleszczyki, as well as the Zaolzie region. I have never been to Zakopane (what a monster.) I am not drawn to Polesie, the seashore or the Bialowieza Forest. The river Vistula near Cracow is alien to me. I don't know and don't want to know Gniezno. But I love the Warsaw Vistula, and when cut off from Warsaw I feel fiercely nostalgic.

Warsaw is mine and I am Warsaw's. I'll say more—I am her. Together with her I have rejoiced and I have grieved, her weather was my weather, her rain, her soil mine as well. We grew up together. Lately, we have grown apart to some extent. New streets, new sections have been built which I no longer understood. For years now I've felt like a foreigner at Zoliborz.[10] I feel closer even to Lublin, even to Hrubieszow which I have never seen.

Warsaw has been my workshop; here are my landmarks and my graves.

I recollect a Nativity play from Freta Street and a small puppet show group from Miodowa Street. It was like this:

Beginning at Christmas, construction workers, unemployed at that time of year, used to go from house to house in the wealthier quarters of the city, and when invited inside homes, would put on a show.

A wooden box for a stage, an accordion or a street organ. And up on the stage—puppets: king Herod on the throne, the devil with a pitchfork.

The show was usually presented in the kitchen so that mud should not be carried from the street to the living room. The cook would put away smaller items so they wouldn't be stolen. On one occasion, two silver spoons

10. A new section of Warsaw.

from a set had disappeared. But the whole thing was beautiful, and scary, and instructive.

When it was over, an old man with a sack appeared to take up collection.

Father always told me to drop the small new silver coins into the old man's sack, and I for my part would change all the cash I had into tiny two-penny coins and, trembling with excitement, toss them into the sack. And the old man would peer inside, shake his long white beard and say:

"Very little, very little, young gentleman, a bit more."

At that time my father took me to a Nativity play.

I recall the long hall of the orphanage, the curtain, the air of mystery, the crowded seats, the expectation.

There were some odd creatures dressed in blue aprons and white caps wearing stiff angels' wings.

I was scared. I was choking with tears.

"Don't go away, daddy."

"Don't be afraid."

A mysterious, strange lady told me to sit in the front row.

Don't ever do that if a child does not want it. I would have much rather sat somewhere to the side, even if others got between me and the stage, even if I was to be crushed and uncomfortable.

Helplessly:

"Daddy!"

"Stay there, silly boy!"

On the way over, I kept asking whether Herod and the devil would be there.

"Wait and see."

This kind of adult reticence is a terrible thing. Don't force surprises on the children if they don't want them. They should be told beforehand, be warned if there's to be any shooting, and if so then when and what kind.

After all, a long, dangerous journey requires preparation.

Only one thing is on the adults' mind:

"Don't forget to peepee before we go, you can't go over there."

But I happen to be busy just now, and I don't want to, anyway. I simply can't do it "just in case."

I knew this would be somehow a more important mystery show and a hundred times more marvelous, even without the old man with a sack taking collections.

Better, in fact, without the old man.

As I have said, it was an instructive hour. Yes. The old man. And not only the old man, but he in particular.

He was insatiable.

Into his sack went first the less important parental coins, then my own, laboriously saved coppers. Taught by bitter, degrading experience, I saved them up for a long time in any way I could. Often a real old beggar in the street suffered because of this, as I thought to myself:

"I won't give it to him, I'll save it for my old man with the sack in the Nativity play."

That old man was insatiable, and his sack bottomless. The sack was very little, a fifth of the size of my purse, yet it absorbed, devoured, wrought out every last penny.

I gave and gave, and I tried again, to see if maybe finally he'd say—enough.

Daddy! Granny! Catherine, I'll pay you back, please lend me a few coins! I'll give you my whole year's allowance.

I was curious. Perhaps I'd be able to catch him disappear for a moment behind the stage and then go on to insist and collect again.

And I was worried and upset by the sad realization

that after the old man there comes the end of the play, that there's nothing more.

Worse: that there's the wearisome ritual of washing before going to bed, maybe even cod-liver oil? On such very special days children should be spared some duties, and not be irritated by all the things that history, study, experience have appropriately advised for the benefit of children. They should have a day's vacation.

Total concentration, total freedom, a complete fairy-tale world woven into a drab existence.

The old man from the puppet show on Miodowa Street—a street so dreadfully changed after the siege of Warsaw—had taught me a great deal. The hopelessness of defense against persistent request and unbounded demands that are impossible to meet.

At first, you give eagerly, then less enthusiastically, from a sense of duty, then, following the laws of inertia, from habit and without heart, and then resentfully, angrily, with despair.

And he wants all that is yours, and you yourself as well.

I hold on to the old man in the puppet show as a last thread linking me with that enchanting fairy tale, with the splendid mysteries of life, the magic of the high-colored, festive thrills.

All this is gone—forever. Finished—buried. That special one, that peculiar [. . .] And this his frightening. The good, the evil.

The ardent desire, impotence, multiplicity, nothingness.

Perhaps I can tell you now how I fed sparrows forty years later.

Don't refuse a child if he asks you to tell the same story over and over and over again.

106

To many children, more perhaps than we realize, a performance should consist of one theme repeated time after time.

A single spectator is frequently a large and responsive audience. Your time will not be wasted.

Old nannies and construction workers are often better pedagogues than a doctor of psychology.

And indeed, the adults, too, cry "Encore!"

Encore!

The same fairy tale endlessly repeated, like a sonata, a favorite sonnet, like a sculpture without the sight of which the day seems colorless.

Picture galleries are quite familiar with the phenomenon of a maniac on the subject of some particular item in an exhibit.

Mine are *San Juan* by Murillo at the Vienna Museum and two sculptures in Cracow by Rygier—*Craft* and *Art*.

Before one slips to the very bottom and becomes reconciled to the shoddy nature of one's emotions . . . one struggles, suffers . . . feels ashamed to be different, inferior to the rest of the crowd, or perhaps only painfully experiences one's own loneliness and alienation?

A puppet show without the old man, not a puppet show but a Nativity play.

It was bad, very bad.

Quite rightly mother was reluctant to entrust her children to the care of her husband, and quite rightly, with a thrill of delight and whoops of joy, we welcomed and long remembered—my sister and I—even the most strenuous, exhausting, unfortunate and deplorable in their outcome "pleasures" sought out with an amazing intuition by that not particularly reliable pedagogue—my father.

He pulled our ears painfully, despite the most emphatic protests from mother and grannie.

"If the child goes deaf, it'll be your doing."

*

The hall was unbearably hot. The preparations dragged on indefinitely . . . The faint sounds and whispers coming from behind the curtain put our nerves on the very edge of endurance. The lamps were smoking. The children pushed and shoved.

"Move over! Take that hand away! Keep your legs to yourself. Don't lean on me."

The bell. And then eternity. The bell. Such feelings might be experienced by a pilot under attack when he has run out of ammunition but has still an important assignment to fulfill. There is no going back and no will, desire or thought of going back.

I don't think the analogy is out of place.

It had begun. Something unrepeatable, unique, final.

I have no recollection of the people. I don't even know whether the devil was red or black. Black, more likely, and he had a tail and horns. He was not a puppet. A live devil. Not a child in disguise.

A child in disguise?

Only grownups could believe in such childish stories.

King Herod himself addresses him as:

"Satan!"

And such a laugh, such leaps, and a real tail, and such "No!" and such a pitchfork, and such "Come here!" I have never seen, never heard before and I even suspected, which may well be true, that hell does really exist.

Everything was authentic. The lights go off, there's cigarette smoke, coughing—that is disturbing.

Miodowa and Freta Streets. And on Freta stood Szmurlo's school. There they used the switch on the children. That too was authentic. But absolutely without comparison.

*

Four o'clock

I have drawn the curtain open in one window only, so as not to wake up the children.

Reginka has *erythema nodozum.*[11]

Probably unwisely I have administered today salicylate 10.0 per 200.0, a tablespoonful every two hours, until she heard ringing in the ears and saw yellow. But yesterday she vomited twice. The lumps on her legs, however, are turning pale, small and no longer hurt.

I have a dread of anything connected with rheumatism in children.

Salicylate—so they said in Paris—and who: no less than Hutinel, Marfan and, oddly enough, Baginski in Berlin.[12]

· Never mind the vomiting. But enough to bring the unfortunate doctor back again if, of course, he says that this is caused by the medication.

As for me, after the Nativity play I had fever for only a couple of days. And in fact only one night. The fever was not perhaps so high but was emphasized sharply by my mother so that a determined "No!" could be administered at least until spring should father care to bring home ice cream.

I am not certain whether on our way back we did not stop to have ice cream or soda ice with pineapple juice.

11. Rheumatic rash.
12. All three well-known pediatricians of France and Germany.

Artificial ice was not yet known at the time and natural ice was easily available in wintertime. So we were able to cool off after the heat.

I remember that I had lost my scarf.

And I also remember that while I was still in bed for the third day and my father came over toward me, my mother admonished him sternly:

"Your hands are cold. Don't come near him!"

Withdrawing meekly, father threw me a conspiratorial glance.

I answered with a cunning, knowing grin, corresponding to something like:

"Sure thing."

I think we both felt that in the last resort not they—mother, grannie, the cook, sister, the maid and the governess, Miss Maria, that stern regiment of women—hold the upper hand, but we, the men.

We are the masters. But we give in for the sake of peace.

Curiously, during my rather long but not particularly varied practice as a doctor, I was frequently called in by the fathers. But never more than once.

Now the mothers were giving in for the sake of peace.

Let me still tell the story of [. . .]

A comment, or rather a hint, to those who some thirty years from now will be drawing up radio programs:

Devote one hour, half to the grandson, half to the grandfather (or father)—to let them chat about "My day yesterday," "How I spent my day yesterday." The beginning would always be the same:

"Yesterday I woke up at . . . I got up . . . Got dressed."

These chats would teach how to view, how to articulate current events, how to eliminate and how to emphasize, how to experience life, how to evaluate it and treat it lightly, to attack it and to succeed—how to live.

Actually, why not also have talks between women, between a teacher and a pupil, a workman and his employer, a clerk and his customer, a lawyer and his client?

It requires experimentation.

Epilogue.

The Polish language knows no such word as "homeland." Fatherland is too much and it is difficult.

Is one only a Jew or perhaps a Pole as well? Perhaps not fatherland but a little house with a garden?

Does not a peasant love his fatherland?

It's just as well that my pen has almost run dry. I have a hard day ahead of me.

Postscript

Ugolino-Dante. They're all right, I suppose. The puppet show . . . If they were alive, they'd know what's right.

There were years when I kept mercuric chloride and morphine pills hidden in the far corner of a drawer. I would take them out only when I went to my mother's grave at the cemetery. But since the start of the war, I have kept them in my pocket, and it's interesting that they were not confiscated when I was searched in jail.

There can be nothing (no experience) more loathsome than an unsuccessful attempt at suicide. This sort of plan should be fully matured so as to ensure absolute certainty of success.

If I kept on postponing my otherwise fully thought-out

111

plan, it was because always at the very last moment some new daydream would sweep me away and could not be abandoned before I worked it out in detail. These were something like themes for short stories. I put them under a common heading of: "Oddities".

Thus:

I invented a machine (I made a detailed design of the whole complicated mechanism). Something in the nature of a microscope. The scale—one hundred. If I should turn the micrometer screw to ninety-nine, everything would die that did not contain at least one percent of humanity. The amount of work was unbelievable. I had to determine how many people (living beings) would go out of circulation each time, who would take their place, and what would be the outcome of such a purged, tentative new life. After a year's deliberations (at night, of course) I came half way with the distillation. Now the only people left were half-beasts, all others have perished. How minutely, to the last detail I planned everything—the best proof that my own person was completely excluded from this peculiar system. By a mere turn of the micrometer screw of my "microscope" I could have taken my own life. What then?

I confess with some embarrassment that I return to this theme today, too, on the more difficult nights. Nights in prison have produced the most interesting chapters of my tale.

There was about a dozen of these daydreams in the workshop to choose from.

Thus . . .

I have found the magic word. I am the ruler of light.

I would fall asleep so full of mental anguish that a protest would rise within me.

"Why me? What do you want of me? There are others,

younger, wiser, more pure, more suitable for this mission?

Leave me to the children. I'm not a sociologist. I'll mess up everything, disgrace both the project and myself."

For rest and relaxation I moved to the children's hospital. The city is casting children my way, like little sea shells—and I am just good to them. I ask neither where they come from, nor for how long or where they are going, for good or evil.

The "Old Doctor" doles out candy, tells stories, answers questions. Dear, tranquil years remote from the tawdry marketplace of the world.

A book, a visit from a friend—and always some patient who needs particular care for several years.

Children recover, or die—as always in a hospital.

I did not philosophize. I did not try to analyze a topic which I already knew through and through. Indeed, for the first seven years I was simply a modest resident physician in a hospital. But for the rest of my years I was bothered by the unpleasant feeling that I had deserted. I had betrayed the sick child, medicine and the hospital. I was carried away by false ambition: to become a doctor and a sculptor of the child's soul. The soul. No more, no less. (Oh, you old fool, you've messed up your life and your cause! You got what you deserved!) A woman, a hysterical slob with the mentality of a charwoman, now represents this important sphere of life, and a *maître d'hôtel* dabbles in hygiene.

Is this why I struggled, often hungry, through the clinics of three European capitals? Ah, what's the use.

*

I don't know how much of this autobiographical stuff

I've already scribbled down. I cannot bring myself to read it and examine the overload. And I'm increasingly in danger of repeating myself. What's even worse, the facts and experiences may be, must be and will be told differently each time as regards the details.

But never mind. It only proves that the moments to which I constantly return were experienced deeply.

And it proves that reminiscences hinge on our immediate experience. Reminiscing, we lie unconsciously. This is an obvious fact and I mention it only for the benefit of the most primitive reader.

One of my frequent daydreams and plans was a trip to China.

This could have materialized, even quite easily.

My poor four-year-old Iuo-Ya from the Japanese war period. I wrote a dedication for her in Polish.

She was extraordinarily patient in teaching Chinese to an inept pupil.

Indeed, there ought to be institutes of Oriental languages. Yes, and professors and lectures.

But everyone would have to spend a year in this kind of village in the Orient and pursue a preliminary course of study under a four-year old.

My German was taught to me by Erna. Walter and Friede were already too old for that, already too grammatical, influenced by novels, textbooks, the school.

Dostoyevski says that with time all our dreams come true, only in such degenerated form that we don't recognize them. I can now recognize my dream of the prewar years.

Not that I went to China. China came to me. Chinese famine, Chinese orphan misery, Chinese mass child mortality.

I do not want to dwell on that subject. To describe

someone else's pain resembles thieving, preying upon misfortune, as if there were not enough of it as things are.

The first newsmen and officials from America did not hide their disappointment: things are not *that* bad. They were looking for corpses and skeletons in the orphanages.

When they visited the Children's Home, the boys were playing at soldiers. With paper caps and sticks.

"Obviously the war hasn't upset them too much," said one ironically.

"That's the way it is now. But the appetites have increased and the nerves have grown numb; something is happening at last. Here and there you can see even toys in the shop windows and so much candy—from ten groszy up to a whole zloty."

"I saw it with my own eyes: a tiny tot scrounged ten groszy and promptly spent it on candy."

"Don't put that in your newspaper."

I've read somewhere: nothing is easier to get used to than the misfortune of others.

When we marched to East Prussia through Ostroleka[13] a woman shopkeeper asked us:

"What's going to happen to us civilians? There's no reason why we should suffer. It's different for you officers, you know you're going to certain death."

Only once did I ride in a rickshaw in Harbin. Now in Warsaw, I recoiled from it for a long time.[14]

A rickshaw runner does not live more than three years, a strong one—five.

I didn't want to have any hand in it.

13. During World War I.
14. Korczak refers to the use of man-drawn vehicles in Warsaw during World War II.

But now I say:

"One must help them earn a living. Better I than two fat profiteers with packages in the bargain."

It is an unpleasant moment when I try to pick the healthier, the stronger-looking (when I'm in a hurry). I always give fifty groszy more than what they ask.

How noble—then and now.

When sharing a room with the healthy children, whenever I lit a cigarette I told myself:

"Smoke is a good expectorant. It's good for them."

*

Five glasses of raw alcohol mixed half and half with hot water gives me inspiration.

Then comes a blissful feeling of weariness without pain, when the scar no longer counts, and neither does the muscle ache in the legs, or even the sore eyes and the burning in the scrotum.

I draw my inspiration from the awareness that I'm lying in bed and so I will remain until morning. Thus for twelve hours the lungs, heart and mind will work normally.

After a busy day.

A taste of sauerkraut and garlic in my mouth, and of the candy I've put in the glass with the spirits to make it more palatable. An epicurean!

And that's not all! Two teaspoons of real coffee grounds with ersatz honey.

The odors: ammonia (urine decomposes quickly now, and I don't rinse the bucket every day), the smell of garlic, of carbide and from time to time of one of my seven roommates.

I feel content, calm and safe. Of course, the tranquillity may be disturbed by Miss Stefa coming in with some piece of news, a problem, a desperate decision.

Or by Miss Esterka, to tell me that someone is crying and can't fall asleep because of a toothache. Or Felek, about a letter to that dignitary which has to go out first thing in the morning.

Just now a moth has flown by, and all at once, anger, inner ferment. Bedbugs—the once infrequent visitors—and now moths, our most recent enemies, let's say enemies number five, but, damn it, that's a subject for tomorrow. Now, in the silence of the night (ten o'clock), I want to go over this day. A busy workday, as I've said.

Apropos of vodka: it was the last half-liter bottle from the old allotment. I did not intend to open it. Kept it for a rainy day. But Satan never sleeps—the sauerkraut, the garlic, the need for consolation, and five decagrams of sausage.

It's so peaceful and safe. Yes, even safe. I don't expect any visit from the outside. Of course, there may chance such a visitor as fire, air-raid, or plaster falling from the ceiling. But the very definition "sense of safety" shows that subjectively I take myself as living deep behind the front lines. He who has no knowledge of the front lines will not understand this.

I feel content and I want to write for a long time, until the pen runs dry. Let's say until one, and then have six full hours of rest.

It even makes one want to joke.

"All's fine," said a not quite sober cabinet minister at not quite the right moment because famine and typhus were ravaging throughout the villages and the graph of fatal tuberculosis cases was rising sharply.

Afterward, political opponents picked on him in the pages of newspapers which call themselves independent.

"All's fine," I say, and it's my wish to be merry.

An amusing reminiscence:

Five decagrams of so-called smoked sausage now costs 1 zloty 20. It used to cost only 80 grosze (and bread a bit more).

I said to a saleswoman:

"Tell me, dear lady, isn't that sausage by chance made from human flesh? It's rather too cheap for horsemeat."

And she replied:

"How should I know. I wasn't there when it was being made."

No sign of annoyance, no friendly smile for a witty customer, no shrug to denounce the joke as nightmarish, macabre. Nothing. She merely stopped slicing, waiting for me to make up my mind. A sorry customer, a sorry joke or implication, not worth talking about.

The day began with weighing the children. The month of May has brought a marked decline. The previous months of this year were not too bad and even May is not yet alarming. But we still have two months or more before the harvest. No getting away from that. And the restrictions imposed by official regulations, new additional interpretations and overcrowding are expected to make the situation still worse.

The children's weighing hour on Saturday is one of big excitement.

After breakfast comes the school meeting.

Breakfast itself also amounts to work. It seems that, following my nasty letter to the dignitary, we have received a fairly good supply of sausage, even ham, even a hundred buns.

Never enough, but although it doesn't amount to much "per head" it has an effect.

Then, even a surprise in the form of two hundred kilograms of potatoes.

An echo of the letters. But there is a rub to it. A passing diplomatic victory, an easily won concession should not give rise to exaggerated hopes and lull vigilance.

They will try one way or another to get their own back—how to stop them? From where will the clouds roll in? What invisible ohms, volts, neons will add up into a thunderclap, into an approaching desert wind, and when?

The gnawing: "Have I done right or wrong?" A gloomy accompaniment to the children's carefree breakfast.

After breakfast, on the run, *à la fourchette*—the toilet (just in case, therefore a bit of a struggle), and a meeting to discuss the school's summer program of leaves and substitutes.

It would be convenient if it could be arranged the same way as last year. But a lot has changed since, a different situation in the dormitories, many newcomers and departures, new promotions, things are—why keep on about it—different. And we would like things to be better.

After the meeting, the school newspaper and court decisions. Thefts have occurred. Not everyone is willing to listen carefully for a good hour to the subject of who has managed well and who badly, what has been received and what is missing, what to expect, what to do. The school newspaper will be a revelation to the new children.

But the oldtimers know that in no way will they learn that which is important, most important to them. In fact, no one is interested, no one listens, so why bother?

Immediately after the newspaper, tiring for me who can reasonably acquiesce in and cunningly turn a blind

119

eye to what is more convenient not to see, when one will not use violence if persuasion is impossible— immediately after the newspaper, a longish conversation with a lady using her influence to get a child admitted. This is an intricate business, calling for caution, pleasantness and firmness. You can go absolutely crazy. But about that some other time. The gong has sounded for dinner.

Whether this Saturday's dinner differs in any way from others I'm not sure, so I prefer to put that off, too.

I am planning for today only three addresses and three calls. Looks easy.

1. To call on a supporter after his illness.

2. A talk on yeast for children in a house almost next door.

3. Close by, a welcome to returnees from the east, kind, friendly people whom I wish well.

That's about it, ha . . .

The first call was to amount to a continuation of the morning discussions on the school.

He wasn't home.

"Please convey my belated greetings. I intended to come sooner, but couldn't make it."

One gets tired of thinking—too many thoughts.

And that elderly man, odd and atypical as primary school teacher; what do I know about him? We've not had a longer talk, or maybe no talk of any kind for a whole year.

There wasn't time? I'm lying. (I can no longer keep my eyes open. I can't, really. I'll wake up and finish it later.

. . . Welcome—the beautiful silence of the night.)

I did not wake up, and in the morning letters had to be written.

Continued the next night

Blessed be peace and quiet.

Nota bene. Last night only seven Jews were shot, the so-called Jewish Gestapo men. What can this mean? It's pointless to delve into it.

An hour's lecture on yeast. Brewers' or bakers', active or inactive? How long it should set? How much to take a week and how often?

Vitamin B.

We shall need five liters per week. But how? Through whom? From where?

A lecture on national foods—during the third call. How kugel and cholent were made in his childhood.

An explosion of the old man's reminiscences. It seems that they returned from hell to the Warsaw paradise.

Why not.

"You're just a kid yourself, in age and experience. You don't know anything."

And then the cholent.

Many a time while in Kiev I remembered the tripe, Warsaw style, and wept from longing for my homeland.

He listened and nodded.

At the front entrance I was stopped by the janitor of the house.

"Help, Almighty! Don't let them question us, ask us anything, tell anything."

The body of a dead boy lies on the sidewalk. Nearby, three boys are playing horses and drivers. At one point they notice the body, move a few steps to the side, go on playing.

Anyone who is a little better off must help his family. A family means his and his wife's brothers and sisters, their brothers, sisters, old parents, children. They give between five and fifty zlotys—and so it goes, day in, day out.

If someone is starving and happens to find relatives willing to acknowledge kinship and ensure two meals a day, he will be happy for two or three days, not more than a week, he will then ask for a shirt, shoes, a decent place to live, some coal. Then medical treatment for himself, his wife and children. Finally—he does not want to be a beggar—he demands employment, a steady job.

It cannot be otherwise, yet it makes one so angry, discouraged, apprehensive and disgusted that even a decent and sensitive man turns against family, all men and himself.

I wish I had nothing, so that they might see it for themselves, and that would be that.

I returned utterly shattered from the "rounds." Seven calls, conversations, staircases, questions. The result: fifty zlotys and a promise of five zlotys a month. To provide for two hundred people!

I stretched out on the bed with my clothes on. The first hot day. I cannot sleep, and at nine a so-called educational session. Occasionally someone will burst out, then withdraw (not worthwhile). Occasionally a meek comment (just for the sake of appearances). The ceremony lasts for an hour. Formality has been satisfied from nine to ten. I exaggerate, of course.

I have special thoughts to fall asleep by. This time: what I could eat without the slightest difficulty, without forcing myself.

Astonishing! I, who only six months ago didn't know

exactly what tasted good (some times that which has pleasant associations).

Raspberries (aunt Magdzia's garden), tripe (Kiev), buckwheat groats (father), kidneys (Paris).

In Palestine, I used to soak every dish in vinegar.

And now, for a soothing subject, what should I have?

The answer:

Champagne with dry biscuits and ice cream with red wine.

A harking back to the time of my throat troubles and no ice cream for twenty years. I drank champagne perhaps three times in my life. Dry biscuits I probably ate as a child when ill.

I put a question to myself:

Perhaps fish with Tartar sauce?

A Wiener schnitzel?

Pâté, rabbit marinated in Malaga with red cabbage.

No! A thousand times no!

Why?

Odd: eating is work, and I am tired.

Sometimes, on waking up in the morning, I think:

"To get up, is to sit on the bed, reach for my underpants, button up, if not all the buttons, then at least one. Struggle into my shirt. Bend down to put on my socks. The suspenders. . . ."

I can sympathize with Krylov who spent all his adult years on a couch, with all his books under it. He would reach for and read the first thing that came to his hand.

I can understand the mistress of P., a friend of mine. She never lit a lamp in the evening but used to read by the light of wax matches which he bought her especially for the purpose.

I have a cough. It's hard to work. To step from the sidewalk down to the street, and then climb up again. A

123

passer-by pushed me inadvertently: I staggered to one side and leaned against a wall.

It's not feebleness. I could easily lift a schoolboy, thirty kilograms of living, resistant weight. It's not strength that's lacking but will. As with a cocaine addict. I have even been wondering if there is not something in the tobacco, the raw vegetables, the air we inhale. For I'm not the only one affected. Sleepwalkers—morphine addicts.

The same with memory.

It happens that I'm on my way to see somebody on important matters. And I stop on the landing:

"What did I come to see him about?" I ponder deeply for some time, and then, with relief: "Oh, yes, I remember. (Kobryner—sickness allowance, Herszaft—extra food rations, Kramsztyk—poor quality of coal and its ratio to the quantity of wood.")

Likewise at meetings. The continuity of discussion is easily broken. Someone interrupts with a remark—and we go off at a tangent for a long time.

What was it we were talking about?

Occasionally, somebody starts off with:

"Firstly. . . ."

You wait in vain for: "Secondly."

Of course, some of us are long-winded, anyway.

A motion:

"The child should be admitted."

Recorded: "Admit." We ought to pass to the next application. No. Not one but three speakers support the motion. At times, it is necessary to intervene more than once.

The discussions keep on "skidding" like a badly driven car.

Wearying, irritating.

Enough!

That's just it: enough! There's no such feeling at the front lines. The front line means orders.

"Ten miles forward, five back—halt—countermarch, bivouac here."

On horseback or a motorcycle—day or night—a brief order penciled on a scrap of paper. It must be carried out, no argument.

Only five undamaged houses left in the village.

Prepare to receive two hundred wounded. They're on their way. Get on with it as best you can.

Here, things are different:

"Please, I'd be so grateful. Would you be so kind?"

You're free not to do it, free to do it some other way, to argue.

In the army the commanding officer may be objectionable. He may harass, discriminate, make senseless demands and, at a critical moment, disappear without having given any orders. And without an order nothing can be done.

Men talk about him, think and dream about him. Not so in civilian life: it's possible to argue, to apply persuasion, to quarrel, to threaten.

The effect is the same.

Boredom.

Boredom in the front lines is short-lived. Already someone is knocking at the door of the peasant hut, a horse has snorted along the road. There's news on the way. Maybe there'll be a move to town, maybe the next night will be spent in a palace, or moving to another front line, or maybe the worst is in store—captivity.

And now, here, we the Jews also don't know what tomorrow holds for us. And yet there's a sense of security. Thus, boredom.

Would you rather be in the battle of Kharkov?

I have brushed aside with scorn all the rubbish printed in the newspapers and I replied:

"I would."

It's worse, perhaps, but different, anyway.

This is why some escape by indulging in trade, others in black marketeering, in social work, in [. . .]

It's daylight again. I yawn. One more day.

That darned tooth that makes my tongue so sore—what a nuisance. I've filed it down, to no avail. Perhaps it's cancer, perhaps my time has come?

May 29, 1942, six in the morning in bed

If you want to check your resistance to madness try to help a shlemiel.

You put the paper right into her hand. She's to deliver it—tomorrow to someone personally—here is the address and the hour. But she's lost the paper or forgot to take it with her, or had no time, or the porter advised her to do something else. She will go tomorrow. It's all the same. Anyhow, she is not sure whether it will be all right. No one to leave the child with, she has some washing to do, just the child's dress.

"Couldn't you leave the washing till tomorrow?"

"It's hot. I promised."

She is upset. Perhaps nothing will come of it? Before the war such things were her husband's problem.

"Perhaps I'm no good, but please don't be angry with me."

I check on the financial situation of a family. They have applied for the admission of their boy.

"He can sleep here. It is quite clean."

126

"You call that clean? You should have seen our place before the war. . . ."

"He could be here with us all day."

"And if it rains?"

"It's not for me to decide. I have recorded my opinion, it is up to the ladies to say what is to be done."

"Doctor! You have no idea what a child he is! You'll see for yourself. You'll be sorry to have only one like him. I had five doctors with me at my confinement."

I do not say: "You're being silly."

I did say that once thirty years back to a mother in the hospital.

She answered: "If I were rich, I wouldn't be silly."

I say to another woman:

"Even Rothschild doesn't give his child more than five meals a day."

"His child will have enough to eat all his life."

I say:

"If your child needed to drink tea, God would have given you milk in one breast and tea in the other."

"If God would only give children what He can give, and what they need. . . ."

I say:

"If you don't believe me, you may call another doctor whom you trust."

"Please, doctor, I don't mean any offense, but how can I trust men if sometimes I don't trust even God?"

A woman says:

"When I had spanked his behind so hard that he seemed to be on fire, I was so sorry for him that, pardon my saying so, I began to cry."

Sami has just brought me a letter to bed: will this do?

"To the Reverend Father, The Vicar of All Saints:

"We kindly request the Rev. Father to grant us permission to come a few times to the church garden on Saturdays, in the morning hours, early if possible (6:30—10 a.m.).

"We long for a little air and greenery. It is stuffy and crowded where we are. We want to become acquainted and make friends with nature.

"We shall not damage the plants.

"Please don't refuse us.

> Zygmus
> Sami
> Abrasza
> Hanka
> Aronek."

How many treasures a man will lose when he no longer has the patience to talk to people with whom he has no business, merely for the sake of getting to know them better.

This application with which we began the day is today a good omen. Maybe I'll collect today more than fifty zlotys.

They sleep in the isolation room. Seven of them. Old Azrylewicz tops the list (*angina pectoris*), Genia (probably lung trouble), Haneczka (asthma). On the other side, Monius, Reginka, Maryla.

Hanka to Genia:

"He has sacrificed so much for her. He would have given his life for her and everything, everything in the world. And she didn't love him, the beast."

"Why beast? Must you love because he loves?"

"That depends how he loves. If he loves just a little, it doesn't matter, but if he is ready to give his life and everything, everything?"

"And did she ask him for anything?"

"Certainly not!"

"Well, you see."

"That's what I mean."

"No, you said she's a beast."

"Because she is."

"I don't want to talk any more."

They were angry at each other.

I feel content and discontent. I become angry, happy, anxious, indignant, I am eager to experience and to avoid experience, I am understanding but I call for punishment by God or man. I judge: this is good, this is bad.

But all this is theoretical. Made to order. Flat, drab, customary, professional; I perceive things as if through a fog, with blotched, non-dimensional emotions. They seem to be beside me, not inside me. I can quite easily give up, postpone, cancel, suspend, substitute.

The sharp tooth cuts into my tongue. I am witness to a revolting scene: I hear words that ought to shock me. I can't cough the phlegm up, my throat is blocked, I suffocate.

A shrug, it's all the same to me.

Indolence. Poverty of feeling, that eternal Jewish resignation: So what? And what next?

"What if my tongue is sore, what if some have been shot?" "He already knows he must die. And what next?" "Surely you cannot die more than once . . .?"

Occasionally, something will rouse me, and I am surprised, seem to realize or recollect that it is so, can be, was once. I see the same thing in others.

A chance meeting with someone we have not seen in many years. In his changed features, we read how different we ourselves have become from our previous lives, from what we were.

And in spite of all, from time to time. . . .

A following scene in the street:

A young boy, still alive or perhaps dead already is

129

lying across the sidewalk. Right there three boys are playing horses and drivers; their reins have gotten entangled. They try every which way to disentangle them, they grow impatient, stumble over the boy lying on the ground. Finally one of them says:

"Let's move on, he gets in the way."

They move a few steps away and continue to struggle with the reins.

Or: I check out an application for a boy to be admitted to the institution. 57 Smocza Street, apartment 57. Two decent families, dying out.

"I don't know if he will be willing to go to the institution right now. He's a good boy. Until his mother dies, too, he will be sorry to leave. The boy is out: he has gone scrounging for food."

The mother is lying on a couch:

"I can't die before he is settled somewhere. Such a good child: he tells me not to sleep in the daytime so as to be able to sleep at night. And at night he says: what are you moaning for, that won't help? You'd better go to sleep."

While the cabmen are quarrelsome, noisy and spiteful, the rickshaw men are gentle and quiet. Like horses or oxen.

On the corner of Solna and Leszno Streets, I notice a group of people consisting of an excited rickshaw man, an enraged peroxide blonde with crinkly hair, a policeman looking somewhat surprised, disappointed. Standing to one side, a smartly dressed woman looks on, evidently shocked. She waits to see how it will all end.

The policeman says gloomily:

"Better give the hooligan what he asks."

And he shuffles on.

The rickshaw man asks a rhetorical question:

"If the lady doesn't want to pay, then I'm a hooligan?"
She:
"I'll pay you two zlotys but you must take me to that house over there."
"You've agreed to three zlotys to the corner of Ciepla Street."
He turns around and rides away, parks in a line of rickshaws.
I asked the shocked elegant woman:
"Do you know what happened?"
"Yes, I was riding with her."
"Who was right?"
"He. But why does he give up two zlotys rather than take her that extra hundred feet?"
"He wants his own way."
"Evidently."
I go up to the rickshaw man.
"What was the trouble?"
"Nothing. I lost two zlotys. So what? I won't be any poorer, and I am a hooligan either way."
I related the incident to three sets of listeners.
I couldn't do otherwise. I simply had to.

One or two fellow workers from Dzielna Street, not without encouragement from a woman not from Dzielna Street, have denounced me to the Jewish Council or Chamber of Health for failing to report cases of typhoid fever. Failure to report even one case may carry a death sentence.
I went to the Health Office and managed to calm them down somewhat and fix things for the future. I wrote two letters to two offices. To one, that I promise and don't keep my promise. To the other I addressed a question: What do they plan to do with me and my new center at Dzielna Street?

The letters were not courteous. Not by any means. But can one justifiably call me a scoundrel?

Now I know: that woman's name is [. . .].

But if she is annoyed at me and a damn nuisance to the hospital system, and I wrote only that about her, then why am I a scoundrel?

What am I expected to do?

A small shopkeeper said to a customer with a complaint:

"My good woman—these are not goods and this is not a store, you are not a customer nor I a vendor, I don't sell to you nor do you pay me because these scraps of paper are not money. You don't lose, and I don't profit. Who would bother to cheat nowadays—for what? Only one's got to do something. Well, am I not right?"

If I were given a missal, I could in a pinch celebrate a mass.

But I should not be able to preach a sermon to the flock in armbands. I should swallow the sentences, read a question in their eyes:

"What now? And what next?"

The words would stick in my throat.

*

Sliska, Panska, Marianska, Komitetowa streets. Memories, memories, memories.

Every house, every courtyard. Here were my half-ruble calls, usually at night.

For medical advice in the daytime to the rich and in the rich streets, I asked three or five rubles. Brazen—as much as Anders, more than Kramsztyk, Baczkiewicz—professorial fees. I, a resident doctor, the general hack, the drudge at the Berson Hospital.

A thick volume of reminiscences.

Jewish doctors had no Christian clientele, only the well placed, living in well-to-do streets. And about these—proudly:

"I was called to the district police chief, the restaurant proprietor, the bank commissioner, the schoolmaster in the high school at Nowolipki Street, the postmaster."

That was already something.

And I had phone calls, not every day, of course:

"Countess Tarnowski would like to speak to you, Doctor. The Prosecutor General of the Judicial Chamber. Madam Tygajlo, wife of a big shot director. The lawyers Makowski, Szyszkowski."

I write down the address on any scrap of paper at hand, asking:

"Would it be all right tomorrow? After the hospital, say, at one. Is there a temperature? Yes, he may have a soft-boiled egg."

Even once:

"General Gilchenko's wife."

And by unimportant contrast: Captain Hopper, a phone call, sometimes two, each time the child had his bowel movement.

Such were the calls of the author of *Drawing-Room Child*,[15] while Goldszmit would go at night to the basement at 52 Sliska Street, to the attic at 17 Panska Street.

I was once called to the Poznanski residence[16] at Aleje Ujazdowskie.

It had to be today. The patients couldn't wait.

"Three rubles," said Dr. Julek, who knew everybody in Warsaw. "They're stingy."

So I went.

"Will you wait a moment, doctor? I'll send for the boys."

15. One of Korczak's early books.
16. Well-known family of textile manufacturers in Poland. (Trans.)

"Are they out?"

"Not far. They're playing in the park. Meanwhile—a cup of tea?"

"I can't spare the time to wait."

"But Doctor Julian always. . . . Have you been writing anything lately?"

"Unfortunately only prescriptions."

The next day:

"For God's sake, my friend!—They're furious. Enemies!"

"I don't give a damn."

"Well, well."

As resident doctor, I had accommodations and an annual salary of 200 rubles, paid quarterly. The house was kept by a good old soul to whom I paid fifteen rubles a month. From private practice I had a hundred rubles a month, and odd sums from articles, too.

I used to spend a lot on cabs.

"A cab to go to Zlota Street? Twenty kopecks? Spendthrift!"

I treated for free the children of socialists, teachers, newspaper men, young lawyers, even doctors—all progressive men.

Sometimes I phoned:

"I won't come till evening. I must bathe and change—we've quite a few cases of scarlet fever. I'd hate to infect the kid."

The kid!

This was the bright side.

And the shadows . . .

I declared:

"Since the older doctors don't want to be bothered at night, especially for the poor, I, being young, must hasten on these errands of mercy."

You understand. Immediate help. How else? What if the child does not last till morning?

Hospital attendants have declared war and they acquired drug wholesalers and two hostile pharmacies as allies.

The unanimous opinion—he is mad. A dangerous lunatic. They differed only in prognosis: is it curable?

Once, at night, a woman in a head scarf came to my door. It was pouring rain.

"My mother's ill."

"But I only treat children."

"She's gone all childish. I know you can't help so why do I bother? But the doctors don't want to write a death certificate. But she's my mother. And without a doctor?"

I went.

"I beg your pardon, I didn't know that you only treat children. Assistant Surgeon Blucharski sent me. A Jew, but a decent man. He said: 'My good woman, you'd have to pay me a ruble because it's a night call. But there's a doctor in the hospital—he'll come for nothing, and still leave some money for medicine'."

Out of spite, I had been signing prescriptions without the Dr.—doctor.

They would say:

"We don't know any doctor by that name, he's probably an orderly."

"But . . . a doctor in the hospital."

So:

"The medicine was prescribed by Dr. NK (not known, improper medicine)."[17]

I used to take twenty kopecks because "it is written in the Talmud that an unpaid doctor is no help to a sick man."

17. Father unknown.

For the most part I found the patients amusing. Funny people. Occasionally annoying.

The night bell. The ambulance brings a child suffering from burns.

"What do you think?"

"I don't. Nothing can be done."

"This is no ordinary child. I am a merchant. I have a house. I can pay."

"Please don't shout. Please leave, you'll wake the patients."

"What's that to me?"

The orderly and I took him under the arms, and out onto the stairs. The bed with the child in it was rolled into the surgery on the ground floor.

"You've got a telephone so you can summon as many Warsaw professors as you like!"

"I'll write to the papers about you. You'll be struck off the roll."

A night ruined.

Or: six o'clock in the morning. A woman enters my room.

"Come to see my child."

I'm still drowsy after a bad night.

"What's wrong with him?"

"Inflammation after scarlet fever."

"Who has been treating him?"

"Various people."

"Then you'd better call those various people."

"And what if I prefer you? I can pay."

"I don't go out at night."

"Is six in the morning night?"

"It's night."

"So you're not coming?"

"No."

Banging the door, she threw a final:

"An aristocrat! You just lost three rubles."

Without bargaining, she would have given me 25 kopecks, and three kopecks "for the janitor." She wanted to punish me: now he won't be able to sleep, chewing his fingers, furious with himself.

He's lost three rubles.

This is my native district Panska Street, Sliska Street.

I've abandoned the hospital for the Children's Home. I have a guilt complex.

Once I had to leave (because of the war).

The second time—a year in Berlin.

The third time—for less than six months, in Paris.

Toward enlightenment, toward knowledge.

Now that I know that I don't know and why I don't know, now that I can act in accordance with the supreme rule "don't harm the sick," I set out for unknown waters.

The hospital has given me a great deal, and I, ungrateful, have given it so little. An ugly desertion. Life has taken revenge.

Yesterday I went to Grzybow No. 1 to collect a donation. The last building before the ghetto wall. A Jewish policeman was killed here yesterday. They say he was signaling to smugglers.

"That's not the place for wholesale business," a neighbor explained.

The store is closed.

The people are scared.

Yesterday, in front of the house, the janitor's assistant: "Doctor, you don't remember me?"

"Wait . . . of course, Szulc!"

"You do remember . . . ?"

"Ah, I remember you too well. Come, tell me." We sat down on the church steps.

My goodness, Grzybow: here in 1905 Sobotka was wounded.

Two recollections intermingled. Bula is forty by now. Not long ago, he was ten.

"I have a child. Come and have some cabbage soup with us. You'll see him."

"I'm tired, I'm on my way home."

We talked for fifteen minutes, perhaps half an hour. Shocked Catholics wearing armbands[18] stole discreet glances in our direction. They know me.

In broad daylight on the church doorstep Korczak is sitting with a smuggler. The children must need money badly. But why so openly, demonstratively, and, however you look at it, shamelessly?

It's a provocation. What would the Germans think if they saw this? Yes: the Jews are brazen and irritating.

And Szulc confides in me:

"In the morning, he has half a pint of milk, a roll and butter. That costs a pretty penny."

"What for?"

"He must know he's got a father."

"A rascal?"

"And why not. He's my son."

"And your wife?"

"A fine woman."

"Do you quarrel?"

"Been together for five years, never raised my voice at her once."

"And do you still remember?"

A suspicion of a smile.

"I think of the Children's Home often. Sometimes I dream about you and Madam Stefa."

"Why didn't you ever come during all these years?"

"When I was well off, I had no time. When I was down and out, how could I come—ragged and dirty?"

18. Catholics of Jewish descent.

"Do you ever see Lejbus?"

"No."

He helped me up. We kissed warmly, heartily.

He was too honest for a crook. And perhaps the Children's Home had sown some seed in him, and trimmed something down? All the time I believed that he had either gotten rich or was no more.

"My partner is rich."

"He helps you a bit?"

"Not he."

How quickly the hours pass. Just now it was midnight—and already it's three in the morning. I had a visitor in my bed.

Mendelek had a bad dream. I carried him to my bed. He stroked my face (!) and went to sleep.

He squeals. He's uncomfortable.

"Are you asleep?"

"I thought I was in the dormitory."

He stares surprised with his black monkeylike beads of eyes.

"You were in the dormitory. Do you want to go back to your own bed?"

"Am I in your way?"

"Lie down at the other end. I'll bring you the pillow."

"Fine."

"I'll be writing. If you're frightened, come back."

"O.K."

Also a grandson. The youngest Nadanowski.

Jakub has written some sort of poem about Moses. If I don't read it today, he may feel hurt.

With satisfaction and melancholy, I am reading his and Monius's diaries. Differing in age, and even more in intellect, in style of life—yet emotionally alike.

Men of broad expanse, of equal level.

There was a strong wind and dust yesterday. Passers-by squinted and covered their eyes.

I remember a scene observed during a sea voyage. A little girl stood on the deck. A sapphire sea in the background. There was a sudden gust of wind. She closed her eyes and covered them with her hands. However, curious, she looked up and—amazing!—the wind was clean, for the first time in her life. Nothing to get into their eyes. She tried it twice before she felt reassured, and she rested her elbows on the rail. And the wind caressed and combed her hair. Boldly she opened her eyes as wide as possible. Embarrassed, she smiled.

"There is such a thing as wind without dirty dust but I didn't know about it. I didn't know there was pure air anywhere in the world. And now I know."

A boy said to me when he left the Children's Home:

"Were it not for the home I wouldn't know that there are honest people in the world who never steal. I wouldn't know that one can speak the truth. I wouldn't know that there are just laws in the world."

The program for this Sunday.

In the morning, 39 Dzielna Street.[19] On the way, see Kohn.

I received a notice to pay a fine following the case I

---

19. Here the municipal orphanage was moved from Plocka Street and was taken over by the Jewish Council. This orphanage was turned into a kind of children's rescue station: sick, abandoned children were collected on the streets and brought there. The number of deaths gives an idea of the conditions and the situation: ten to fifteen deaths daily. The Doctor took upon himself to reform this "pre-funeral home," as he called it. The depraved personnel did everything possible to fight the new curator, and the council administration was not too cooperative either (when, for example, Korczak requested a twenty thousand zloty grant, they offered him one thousand). No wonder Korczak had to pay with his health for every day spent at this institution.

had. Five hundred zlotys a month. So, including today (June 1), I ought to pay fifteen hundred zlotys. Should I default, the whole amount, three or five thousand—I don't remember exactly—would be payable at once. The point is that I want them to accept my savings book with 3000 zlotys. I suggested this when they asked me at Szuch Avenue[20] whether the Jewish community office would not pay bail for my release.

"Don't you want the community office to pay for you?"

"No."

It was then that they wrote down that I had 3000 zlotys in a savings book.

Several weeks, rich in developments, have gone by.

I stopped writing because Heniek was sick, and I thought there was nobody to type up my nightly revelations.

Curiously enough, I believed that to be true, although I knew that several other boys could do it equally well.

It would have been a different matter if I had decided to make writing a daily duty. As during the war. *How To Love a Child* was typed even during halts of a few hours. At Jeziorna, even Walenty rebelled.[21]

"Is it worthwhile for just half an hour?"

And then in Kiev, too, it was absolutely every day.

And now I am finishing my pad. Another excuse to write no more tonight, though I feel perfectly rested. I had four cups of strong coffee, prepared from dregs, it's true, but reinforced I suspect with fresh-ground coffee.

We do deceive ourselves: I have no more paper. I shall read Diderot's *Jacques le fataliste*.

20. Gestapo headquarters in Warsaw. (Trans.).

21. It appears that during World War I Korczak's orderly objected to his notes, which deprived him of rest.

Probably for the first time I have forgotten that I am living through my tenth seven-year life stage, 7×9.

Tensely, I waited for 2×7. Perhaps it was precisely then that I had heard of this for the first time.

The Gypsy's seven, seven days of the week. Why not the victorious ten of olden days (the number of fingers)?

I remember the tense feeling as I waited for the clock to strike midnight. The change was supposed to take place just at that instant.

There was some scandal with a hermaphrodite. I am not sure whether it was exactly at that time. I don't quite know whether I was afraid that I might wake up to find I was a girl. I made up my mind that if that happened I would keep it secret at all costs.

Gepner[22] 7×10, I—7×9. If I go over my life, the seventh year of age brought me a sense of my own value. I exist. I have·weight. I have meaning. I am visible. I can. I will.

Fourteen. I look around. I perceive. I see. . . . My eyes were due to open. They did. My first ideas concerning education reforms. I read a lot. My first anxieties and frustrations. Now, imagined voyages and stormy adventures, then again a quiet family life, friendship (love) for Stach. The primary dream among many, among many dozens: he's a priest, I a doctor in that small town. I thought of love, formerly I only felt it, I loved. From seven to fourteen I was permanently in love, always with a different girl. Odd, but I remember many of them. The two sisters from the skating rink, Stach's cousin (her grandfather was Italian), the one in mourning, Zosia Kalhorn, Anielka, Irenka from Naleczow. Stefcia for whom I used to pick flowers from the beds by the fountain in Saski Park. Then that little tightrope dancer, I

---

22. A well-to-do philanthropist supporting the Children's Home.

grieved bitterly over her fate. I loved for a week, a
month, occasionally two at once, three. One I wanted to
have for a sister, another for a wife, for a sister-in-
law. . . . My love for Mania from my fourteenth year (at
Wawer in summer) was an integral part of that [. . .] of
feelings that alternately gently rocked or violently shook
me. The exciting world was not already behind me. Now
it is within me. I exist not to be loved and admired, but
myself to act and love. It is not the duty of those around
to help me but I am duty-bound to look after the world,
after man.

3×7. In the seventh year, school, in the fourteenth,
religious maturity, in the twenty-first, military service.
For a long time I've had the feeling of being cooped up.
Once I was imprisoned by the school. Now I am gener-
ally shut in. I want to prevail, fight for new areas.

(Probably these thoughts were suggested to me by the
22nd of June when, after the longest day of the year, the
sun sets three minutes earlier each day. Sneakingly, im-
perceptibly but inexorably there is less of the day by
three minutes and again by three, and again. I used to
commiserate with old age and death; now, less sure myself, I begin to fear for my own self. One must fight for
and achieve a great balance in order to have enough to
write off for losses. Perhaps it was precisely then that the
dentist pulled out my first adult tooth which would not
grow again. My rebellion against the law of nature, not
social conditions, came to a head. Get ready, aim, fire.)

4×7. The need for efficient functioning over the limited area of one's own "workshop." I am anxious to
achieve, to know, not to idle, not to stray. I need to be a
good doctor. I shape a model of my own. I do not wish to
model myself upon acknowledged authorities. (Things
used to be otherwise once. Even today there are moments when I feel like a young man with a long road

143

ahead. I find it worthwhile to plan and venture anew. In the second, and certainly in the third seven years, I felt so old at times, that everything was a constant repetition, already too late, not worthwhile. Indeed, life is like a flame. It dies down though there is ample fuel. Suddenly, when it is about to die down, it flares up, sending out sparks and shooting up brightly. And it dies out. A hot day in the fall and the awareness that this is the last, exceptional, cold morning in July.)

5×7. I got my money back in the lottery of life. My number is already drawn. My money back. So I will not lose in this drawing unless I stake again. Might have been worse: I might have lost. But no more chance of the big prize—a pity. Fair enough—I have gotten back what I paid in. Safe. But drab—and regrettable.

Loneliness does not hurt. I value memories. A schoolmate—a friendly chat over a cup of coffee in a quiet corner where no one will disturb us. I seek no friend because I know I will not find one. I do not strive to know more than it is possible. I have signed a pact with life: we will not get in each other's way. It's unbecoming to fly at each other—no use anyway. In politics, I believe, they call it a demarcation of the spheres of influence. So far and no more, no farther, no higher. You and I.

6×7. Perhaps? Already, or not yet? That depends. Let us balance the books. Assets, liabilities. If one knew how many years were left, when the end would come. I do not feel the inner call of death, but already I think about it. When a tailor makes me a new suit, I do not say: that'll be the last. But the office desk and the chest of drawers will surely outlive me. There'll be no wild escapades, no surprises. There'll be more severe or milder winters, rainy and scorching summers. And gratifying coolness, and gales, and dust storms. So I will say: in ten, fifteen years we have not had such hail, such floods. I remember a similar fire. I was young then, let me think—already a university student or still a schoolboy? 7×7. What is life really, what is happiness? So long as it is not worse, just as it is now. Two sevens have met and exchanged polite greetings, glad that things are as they are, and precisely here, and under such specific conditions. A newspaper—seemingly only mindless reading. Perhaps it is. Yet you cannot do without it. There are the editorials, and a novel in installments, obituaries and theatrical reviews, reports from the courts. The movies—a new film. A new novel. Small accidents. Classified advertisements. Not really so interesting as rather offering a choice. Someone killed under the streetcar, somebody has invented something or other, someone's fur coat was stolen, and here a five-year prison sentence. Somebody wants to buy a sewing machine or a typewriter, or has a piano for sale or is looking for a three-room apartment with all modern conveniences. A broad river bed, I should say, of the majestically flowing Vistula River as it flows near Warsaw.

My city, my street, the store where I regularly shop, my tailor, and most important of all—my workshop.

As long as it is no worse. For, if one could say to the sun: stop, probably it should be at this time of life. (There is a small dissertation *On the Happiest Period of Life*—and, believe it or not, by Karamzin.[23] His stuff sure bothered us in the Russian school.)

$7\times8 = 56$. How these years have flown. Literally flown. It seems but yesterday that it was 7×7. Nothing added, nothing subtracted. What a vast difference in the ages: seven and fourteen, fourteen and twenty-one. And for me, at 7×7 and 7×8—absolutely the same.

23. N. N. Karamzin (1766–1826) Russian writer and historian.

Please do not get me wrong. Obviously there are no two identical leaves, nor drops, nor grains of sand. This fellow has a balder head, that one more gray hair. This one has false teeth, that one only caps. This one wears eyeglasses, that one is hard of hearing. This one is more bony, that one is fatter. But I am speaking of the seven-year stages.

I know: life could be divided into five-year periods, and that way, too, it could be made to fit. I know: the living conditions. Wealth, poverty. Success, worries. I know the war, wars, disasters. And this too is relative. A certain lady told me: "The war has spoiled me and later it was very difficult to settle down." Even the present war is spoiling many. Yet surely there is not a man who does not believe that the failures of strength, health and energy spring not from the war but from that 7×8 and 7×9.

What ghastly dreams! Last night: the Germans, I without an armband during a curfew at Praga.[24] I woke up. And again a dream. On a train, I am moved, a meter at a time, into a compartment where there are already several Jews. Again some had died tonight. Bodies of dead children. One dead child in a bucket. Another skinned, lying on the boards in the mortuary, clearly still breathing. Another dream: I am standing high up on a wobbly ladder, and my father keeps on pushing a piece of cake into my mouth, a big lump with sugar frosting and raisins, and anything that falls from my mouth he puts crumbed into his pocket.

I woke up in a sweat at the most crucial point. Is not death such an awakening at a point when there is no apparent way out?

"Every man can surely find five minutes in which to die"—I have read somewhere.

24. The section of Warsaw east of the Vistula.

Summer. 39 Dzielna Street. Abstracts.

When the tenth person in turn pesters me about a decision regarding the candy and the honeycakes—it drives me crazy. Are there no other problems to solve except those of the honeycakes!

Yesterday, a little boy came back from the hospital after having had a leg amputated following frostbite. Everybody thinks it his duty to tell me about it. What annoying thoughtlessness! I'll put up with it. But that boy—a hero of the day?

Too few hysterics around here, it seems.

*

Two sensible, level-headed, unbiased informants and advisers have let me down. The weighing machine and the thermometer.

I have ceased to believe them. They too tell lies.

*

We say:

Group one, group two—area A, area B, area C. We say: the wing. (The wing has not had its breakfast yet.) We say: area U, area I. Group A of boys and girls alternately . . .

Is it incidental, some sort of historical rudiments, or a desire to intimidate and flabbergast a newcomer?

Hard to say.

*

We have various kinds of "men": a barrow man, an errand boy, a porter or janitor. We have women workers, house servants, charwomen, governesses—today a hygienist has emerged. We have section managers, floor or landing stewards, probably keyguards as well. Such things did not bother me in jail, but here it is upsetting.

All this is difficult to grasp.

*

There are women for the morning, the afternoon, the night, ill, convalescent, feverish, temporary, group leaders, half-and-halves, outside workers, the dismissed.

Hard to say who's who.

*

She looks at me with alarm in her eyes and answers: I don't know.

As if she came yesterday, hasn't worked here for ten years but only came yesterday. As if what I am asking related to the North Pole or the equator.

She doesn't know. Just does her job.

The only way: not to interfere and not to know what the hundred-headed roll of employees do.

*

Children?

Not only children but cattle, and carrion, and dung.

I have caught myself in a transgression. I do not give them a full teaspoon of cod liver oil. I think that on their graves will grow nettle, burdock and madwort, not nutritious vegetables and flowers, oh no.

*

I have the impression that they send us here the mere

leavings of children and of staff from allied institutions. An imbecile, a spiteful predator expelled from the Children's Home, has landed here, too. When finally a German soldier intervened in his behalf, I told the policeman that if Fula were to come back I would take his gun and stand guard, and let him, the policeman, take charge of the Home.

So the mother placed him here.

*

The staff.

A chimney sweep must be smeared with soot.

A butcher must be stained with blood (a surgeon, too).

A cesspool cleaner stinks.

A waiter must be crafty. If he is not, woe be unto him.

I feel all smeared, blood-stained, stinking. And crafty, since I am alive—I sleep, eat and, occasionally I ever joke.

*

I have invited for consultation:

Brokman

Mrs. Heller

Przedborski

Gantz-Kohn

Lifszyc

Mayzner

Mrs. Zand[25]

Now advise me: limewater: all right. What else?

*

25. An attorney and several physicians working in the ghetto.

Long after the war, men will not be able to look each other in the eyes without reading the question: How did it happen that you survived? How did you do it?

My dear Anka. . . .

1. I don't make social calls. I go to beg for money, foodstuffs, an item of information, a lead. If you call that social calls . . . they are arduous, degrading work. Must play the clown, too. People don't like gloomy faces.

I often call on the Chmielarz family. They always find some food for me. That's not a social call, either. I see it as a good deed, they—as an exchange of services. In spite of the kind, gentle and soothing atmosphere, it is frequently tiring, too.

Reading as relaxation begins to fail. A dangerous symptom. I am distracted and that itself worries me. I don't want to sink into idiocy.

2. I have sent the 500 zlotys. If I am in any danger, the least from that side, in that case. A reliable and stalwart friend—an excellent lawyer—looks after the matter. I take no steps without his approval.

3. I am going to see the head of the Staff Section. I could not have failed to consider the case since there was none. Whatever Madam Stefa said, promised and undertook, I did not know since no one told me. I have kept the secret.

4. In my humble opinion, I discharge my duties to the best of my ability. I never refuse if I can help it. I have never undertaken to look after cops, so that charge is unjust.

June 26, 1942.

END OF PART ONE

I have read it over. I could hardly understand it. And the reader?

No wonder, that the memoirs are incomprehensible to the reader. Is it possible to understand someone else's reminiscences, someone else's life? It seems that I ought to be able to perceive without effort what I myself write about. Ah, but is it possible to understand one's own remembrances?

*

Slowacki left behind his letters to his mother. They give a vivid picture of his experiences over several years. Because of these letters, a document has survived attesting to his transformation under the influence of Towianski.[26]

It has crossed my mind:

"Perhaps I should write these diaries in the form of letters to my sister?"

Cold, strange, detached was my first letter to her. A reply to her letter.

And here:

"My dear . . ."

. . . .

What a great and painful misunderstanding.

*

Proust is sprawling and overly detailed?
Far from it!

26. Founder of a religious sect among Polish emigrants in France in XIX century. His ideas of Messianism had a great influence on Polish poets and writers of that time.

Every hour—a heavy volume, an hour's reading.
So be it.
You have to read all day to understand a day of mine,
more or less. Week after week, year after year.
And we, during a few hours, just a few hours of our
time, want to relive a whole lifetime.
No way. You may grasp some vague summary in a
careless sketch—a single episode in a thousand, in a
hundred thousand.

I am writing this in the classroom during a Hebrew
lesson.
Zamenhof[27] comes to my mind. Naive, audacious: he
wanted to rectify God's error or God's punishment. He
wanted to fuse the misplaced languages into one again.
Stop!
We must divide, divide, divide. Not fuse.
What would man have?
We must fill his time, give him something to do, a goal
in life.
"He speaks three languages. He is studying a language. He knows five languages."
Here we have two groups of children who have given
up amusement, easy books, chats with friends for a vol-
untary study of Hebrew.
When the younger group finished their hour, one stu-
dent exclaimed with surprise:
"What, an hour has passed already?"
So. "Da" in Russian, "ja" in German, "oui" in French,
"yes" in English, "ken" in Hebrew. Enough to fill not
one but three lives.

___

27. Warsaw physician, the inventor of Esperanto (1859–1917).

PART TWO

Today is Monday. From eight to nine a pupil's hostel chat. Whoever wants to may attend. Provided he does not interrupt.

Suggested themes:

1. The emancipation of women
2. Heredity
3. Loneliness
4. Napoleon
5. What is duty?
6. On the medical profession
7. Amiel's memoirs[1]
8. From the doctor's reminiscences
9. On London
10. On Mendel
11. Leonardo da Vinci
12. On Fabre
13. The senses and the mind
14. The genius and his surroundings (mutual impact)
15. The Encyclopedists
16. How different writers worked
17. Nationality. Nation. Cosmopolitanism
18. Symbiosis
19. Evil and malice
20. Freedom. Destiny and free will.

When I was the editor of "Maly Przeglad,"[2] only two themes attracted young people:

Communism (politics) and sexual problems.

1. French poet who became known when his memoirs were posthumously published (1821–1881).
2. A weekly supplement to the prewar Warsaw daily "Nasz Przeglad."

Wicked, shameful years—destructive, base. Prewar years, lying, hypocritical. Cursed years.

Life was not worth living.

Filth. Stinking filth.

Then the storm came. Cleared the air. Made breathing easier. More oxygen.

*

I devote this tale
to Szymonek Jakubowicz

From the series:
"STRANGE HAPPENINGS"

Let the planet be called Ro, and he be named Professor, Astronomer or whatever you like, And we shall call the place on Planet Ro where Professor Zi was making his observations a laboratory.

The name of the instrument in our imperfect speech will be a bit too long: "astropsychomicrometer," a micrometer in the medium of astral psychical vibrations.

In terms of our terrestrial observatories, the Professor used a telescope which, by buzzing, communicated what was going on here and there in the universe, and possibly the intricate instrument projected pictures onto a screen or recorded vibrations in the same way as a seismograph.

Anyhow, this is unimportant.

What is important is that the scientist from Planet Ro could control psychic energy and could change heat radiation into spiritual, or to be more precise, moral power.

All right. So long as we take morality to be the harmony of impressions and the equilibrium of feelings.

One more comparison comes to mind: a radio that

transmits not songs and music or war communiqués but rays of spiritual order. In the life of stars, and not merely in our own solar system.

Order and tranquillity.

And so Professor Zi sits troubled in his workroom and thinks:

"That restless spark which is Earth is again in ferment. Disorder, disquiet, negative emotions predominate, reign. Miserable, painful, impure is their life over there. Its disorders upset the current of time and of impressions. . . .

"The pointer has wavered again. The line of suffering has gone up violently."

One, two, three, four, five.

Astronomer Zi frowns.

"Should one put an end to this senseless game? This bloody game? The beings inhabiting the earth have blood. And tears. And they moan when hurt. Don't they want to be happy? Are they wandering, unable to find the way? It is dark down there, a gale and a dust storm blinds them."

The pointer quickly records more and more turbulence.

Improperly used steel administers penalty. But at the same time it guides and educates, prepares the proper spirit for new conquests and initiations.

"There are bodies of water upon that distant speck of light. From slaughtered trees you have built floating houses, braced them with steel. What a stupendous effort! You're unruly, indolent, but capable. You have no wings yet. How vast the flying heights and the expanse of oceans must seem to you."

Bzzzz . . . Bzzzz. . . .

"And instead of rejoicing in their hearts, in song with

an intensified collective effort, instead of tying the threads together, they tangle them and tear.

"What am I to do then? To check them would mean to force them onto a road for which they are not yet sufficiently mature, an effort beyond their strength and a goal transcending their present comprehension. No doubt they themselves are doing the same. Slavery, coercion, violence. Things which disturb, provoke and hurt."

Professor Zi sighs. Closes his eyes. Applies the sensor of the astropsychomicrometer to his chest and listens.

And there is a war on earth. Fires, smoldering ruins, battlefields. Man, responsible for the Earth and its products, does not know, or knows but understands for himself alone.

The space over Planet Ro (perhaps Lo) is filled with the blue, with the fragrance of the lily of the valley and the sweetness of wine. Winged feelings flicker like snowflakes, raising a song after a song, gentle and pure.

Our earth is still young. And a beginning is painful labor.

*

From the diaries they bring over for reading.

Marceli writes:

"I have found a penknife. I will give 15 groszy to the poor. I have promised myself."

Szlama:

"A widow sits at home and weeps. Perhaps the older son will bring something from his smuggling. She does not know that a gendarme has shot her son dead. . . . But do you know that soon everything will be all right again?"

Szymonek:

"My father was a fighter for a piece of bread. Although father was busy all day, yet he loved me."

(And two shocking memories.)

Natek: "Chess was invented by a Persian wizard or king."

Mietek: "That siddur[3] which I want to have bound is a souvenir since it belonged to my brother who died, and it was sent to him for the day of his bar mitzvah by his brother in Palestine."

Leon: "I needed a box to keep all sorts of souvenirs. Hersz wanted to sell me a French polished box for 3½ zlotys." (Here follows an involved account of the deal.)

Szmulek: "I have bought little nails for 20 groszy. Tomorrow I will have big expenses."

Abus: "If I sit a bit longer in the toilet, right away they say that I am selfish. And I want to be liked by others." (I know this problem from jail.)

I have fixed a toilet-fee scale:

1. For number one—catch five flies.

2. For number two—second class (a bucket-stool-with-a-hole combination)—ten flies.

3. First class—a toilet seat—fifteen flies.

One of the boys asks:

"May I pay the flies later? I can't wait."

Another:

"You go and do it, go on. . . . I'll catch them for you."

Every fly caught in the isolation room counts as two.

"And does it count if a fly is hit and gets away?" When you've got it, you've got it, there are certainly very few flies. Using the same system, a dozen or so years ago, kindergarten children caught all the bedbugs at Goclawek.

Community good will—what a mighty force.

3. Prayer book.

EUTHANASIA

The church has shrouded in ritual the functions of birth, marriage and death.

The ritual of the mass has taken possession of man's entire spiritual life, controlling even the accessory economic life of the flock.

When men cast away (why so abruptly?) the childish cloth, already tight and too short—artless and repeatedly patched up—the flock—the church expanded into a number of institutions.

Now construction is not only in the service of places of worship. The first, to be sure, was France, Paris who erected the contemporary tower of Babel. Its name is the Eiffel Tower.

There is the building of schools and secular universities, theaters, museums, concert halls, crematoria, hotels, stadiums—huge, magnificent, hygienic, modern.

There are now speeches over the radio, not only a sermon and the priest's address.

There are libraries, printing shops, bookstores, not only a holy book or a scroll on the altar and a street stand with holy objects.

There is the physician—the mighty structure of medicine. Now it is no longer the priest's prayer which protects against disease.

Against hail, and flood, fire and pestilence—there is now health care and insurance companies.

Social welfare replaces the one-time penny for the blind.

Sculpture and paintings on canvas are in art galleries, not only on ceilings and walls of houses of worship.

There are meteorological institutes instead of prayer services.

The hospital has grown out of the church.

All was contained within it and took its beginnings from it.

Now the stock exchange, not the square in front of the church, controls prices.

There are international meetings of learned specialists and countless periodicals, in place of the exchange of private letters and mutual social calls, discussions and feasts of the Levites.

Diplomacy, no less effective than prayers, protects us against the outbreak of war.

The penal, civil, and commercial codes are the equivalent of the old decalogue and its commentaries.

Prisons are former cloisters. Court verdicts—excommunications.

The man of today has matured, but he has not become wiser and gentler.

Once upon a time, everything was within the church, whatever was lofty, solemn, rational, beautiful, humanitarian, humane. Nothing was outside it but the beast of burden, numbed, exploited, helpless.

And even today, even at the very peak of development and knowledge, men have founded their most important affairs upon baptism, the sacraments of marriage, and rites linked with the hour of death for some and inheritance for the survivors.

So very recently, yes, almost yesterday, there appeared at the conference tables: the subject of population and birth control, the discussion on the perfect marriage and—euthanasia.

The right to kill as an act of mercy belongs to him who loves, and suffers—if he himself also does not want to remain alive. It will be this way in a few years.

An odd saying has come into use:

"To be a sociable, a Gypsy has gone to the gallows."

When on my sister's return from Paris I suggested to her that we should commit suicide together, there was no idea or program of bankruptcy involved. On the contrary. I could find no place for myself in the world or in life.

Qui bono that dozen odd years more? Perhaps it was my fault, who knows, that I did not repeat my offer. The deal did not materialize because of the differences of opinion.

When during the dark hours I pondered over the killing (putting to sleep) of infants and old people of the Jewish ghetto, I saw it as a murder of the sick and feeble, as an assassination of the innocents.

A nurse from the cancer ward told me that she used to put a lethal dose of medicine by the bedside of her patients, instructing them:

"Not more than one spoonful, because it's poison. One spoonful will alleviate the pain like medicine."

And over many years, not a single patient has reached for the fatal dose.

How will this problem look in the future?

An official board, what else? A well-developed organization. One big office, small rooms. Office desks. Lawyers, doctors, philosophers, business advisers, of different ages and specialties.

A person submits an application. Everybody is eligible. There are, perhaps, ample restrictions so that applications would not be made without proper consideration or not in earnest, deceitfully taking advantage of the board or to trick one's own family.

An application for death might serve to exert pressure upon the family:

"Come back to me, dear wife, or else—here's a receipt for my death application. . . . Daddy, I need money to have a good time.

"If you don't give me a passing grade in my matricula-
tion, you will suffer pangs of conscience, I'll poison your
peace of mind."

So:

The application must be on a specified kind of paper
only. Say, in Greek or Latin. A list of witnesses is necessary. Perhaps stamps. Perhaps a fee payable in four quarterly installments or three monthly, or seven weekly
installments.

The application must be well substantiated.

"I do not want to live because of a disease, a financial
crash, a disappointment, a surfeit, because my father,
son, friend has failed me.

"I request that the operation be performed within one
week, without delay."

Has anyone ever collected incidents and experiences,
confidences, letters, memoirs from concentration camps,
prisons, from condemned men or those threatened with
a death sentence, on the eve of a big battle, on the stock
exchange, in gambling houses?

The application is accepted. The formalities complied
with. Now comes an examination, conducted along the
same lines as a trial in court.

A medical examination. A consultation with a psychologist. Perhaps a confession, maybe psychoanalysis.

Additional interviews with witnesses.

Fixing the dates, any possible changes.

The specialists and the experts.

There may be a postponment of the implementation of
a favorable decision. Or a trial euthanasia. For it happens
that a man, having once tried the delights and joys of
committing suicide, lives to an advanced age never trying again.

One of the initiation processes for freemasons is said to

163

be such a test consisting of an unsuccessful leap into the unknown.

The place of execution. This is my personal invention—after a cut-off date.

Or:

"Proceed to this or that place. There you will receive the death you applied for. Your request will be granted in ten days' time at a morning, evening hour.

The authorities are requested to assist on land, at sea and in the air."

It looks as if I am joking. But no.

There are problems that lie, like bloodstained rags, right across the sidewalk. People cross to the other side of the street or turn their eyes away in order not to see.

I do the same.

However, where a broad issue and not just one beggar dying of starvation, is involved, this is not allowed. At stake is not merely one or a hundred miserable wretches in a hard year of war but millions through the centuries.

This you must look straight in the face.

My life has been difficult but interesting. In my younger days I asked God for precisely that.

"God, give me a hard life but let it be beautiful, rich and aspiring."

On discovering that Slowacki had done the same, I felt rather pained that it was not my invention, that I had a precursor.

When I was seventeen, I even started writing a novel entitled *Suicide*. The main character hated life out of fear of insanity.

I used to be desperately afraid of the lunatic asylum. My father was sent there several times.

So I am the son of a madman. A hereditary affliction.

More than two score years have gone by, and to this day this thought is at times a torment to me.

I am too fond of my follies not to be afraid that someone may try to treat me against my will.

At this point, I should say: part two. No. I have merely been longwinded. But I don't know how to be more concise.

July 15, 1942

A week's break in writing which, it seems, was absolutely necessary. I had the same feeling when writing *How To Love A Child*. I used to write at stops, in a meadow under a pine tree, sitting on a stump. Everything seemed important and if I did not note it down I would forget. An irretrievable loss to humanity. At times there was a pause for a month. Why make a fool of myself? That which is wise is known to a hundred men. When the proper time comes, they will tell you and act upon whatever is of major importance. It was not Edison who made the inventions; they were hanging as if on a line, like wash drying in the sun. All he did was to gather them off the line.

The same goes for Pasteur, the same for Pestalozzi. It is there. Only it must be expressed.

So it is with every problem.

If not one, then another, will launch himself first into space.

For a long time I could not understand in what way the present-day orphanage differs from the earlier ones, from our own as it once was.

The orphanage—barracks. I know.

The orphanage—prison. Yes.

The orphanage—beehive, anthill. No.

165

The Children's Home is now a home for the aged. I have seven occupants in the isolation room, three of whom are newcomers. The age of the patients ranges from seven right up to Azryl, sixty, who moans sitting on his bed with his legs dangling, and elbows resting on the back of a chair.

The morning discussions of the children are the result of temperature taking. What's my temperature, and what's yours? Who's feeling worse? How did they pass the night?

A sanatorium for rich patients, capricious, affectionately attached to their ailments.

Leon has fainted for the first time in his life. Now he is trying to find the cause.

The children moon about. Only the outer appearances are normal. Underneath lurks weariness, discouragement, anger, mutiny, mistrust, resentment, longing.

The seriousness of their diaries hurts. In response to their confidences I share mine with them as an equal. Our common experiences—theirs and mine. Mine are more diluted, watered down, otherwise the same.

*

Yesterday, while counting the votes of the staff at Dzielna Street, I understood the essence of their solidarity.

They hate one another but none of them will allow the other to come to harm.

"Don't meddle in our affairs. You are a stranger, an enemy. Even if you offer something useful it is only an illusion and will ultimately do harm."

The most devoted nurse, Miss Wittlin, had died—tuberculosis.

Too bad—Wittlin. Two: school and the isolation room.

"The salt of the earth" dissolves—the manure remains.

What will be the upshot?

"It is harder to live a day right than to write a book."

Every day, not just yesterday, is a book—a thick volume, a chapter, enough for many years.

How improbably long a man is alive.

There's nothing absurd about the calculations of the Holy Scriptures: Methuselah really did live about a thousand years.

Night, July 18

During the first week of our last stay at the Goclawek summer home, the result of the consumption of bread of unknown composition and make was a mass poisoning which affected the children and some of the staff.

Diarrhea. The excrements boiled over in the chamber pots. Bubbles formed upon the surface of the pitchlike matter. Bursting they exuded a sweetish-putrid odor, which not only attacked the sense of smell but invaded the throat, eyes, ears, the brain.

Just now we have something similar, but it consists of vomiting and watery stools.

During the night, the boys lost 80 kg among them—on the average a kilogram per head. The girls—60 kg (somewhat less).

The children's digestive tracts worked under heavy strain. Not much was needed to precipitate a disaster. Perhaps it was the inoculation against dysentery (five days ago) or the ground pepper added pursuant to a French recipe to the stale eggs used for Friday's *pâté*.

The next day, not so much as a single kilogram of the losses in weight was made up.

Help for those vomiting, moaning with pain, was administered in near darkness—with limewater. (Unlimited dental chalk for whoever wanted it, jug after jug. In addition, a drug for those suffering from headaches.) Finally, for the staff, sparingly—morphine. An injection of caffein for a hysterical new inmate following a collapse.

His mother, wasting away of ulcerated intestines, was unwilling to die until the child had been placed in the Home. The boy was unwilling to go until the mother had died. He finally yielded. The mother died propitiously, now the child has pangs of conscience. In his illness, he mimics his mother: he moans (screams), complains of pain, then gasps, then feels hot, finally is dying of thirst.

"Water!"

I pace the dormitory to and fro. Will there be an outbreak of mass hysteria? Might be!

But the children's confidence in the leadership prevailed. They believed that as long as the doctor was calm there was no danger.

Actually I was not so calm. But the fact that I shouted at the troublesome patient and threatened to throw him out onto the staircase was evidence that the man at the helm had everything under control. The decisive factor: he shouts, so he knows.

The next day, that was yesterday—the play. *The Post Office* by Tagore. Applause, handshakes, smiles, efforts at cordial conversation. (The chairwoman looked over the house after the performance and pronounced that though we are cramped, that genius Korczak had demonstrated that he could work miracles even in a rat hole.)

This is why others have been allotted palaces.

(This reminded me of the pompous opening ceremony of a new kindergarten in the workers' house at Gorczewska Street with the participation of Mrs. Moscicka[4]—the other one.)

4. Wife of the prewar President of Poland.

How ridiculous they are.

What would have happened if the actors of yesterday were to continue in their roles today?

Jerzyk fancied himself a fakir.

Chaimek—a real doctor.

Adek—the lord mayor.

(Perhaps illusions would be a good subject for the Wednesday dormitory talk. Illusions, their role in the life of mankind. . . .)

And so to Dzielna Street.

*

The same day. Midnight

If I were to say that I have never written a single line unwillingly, that would be the truth. But it would also be true to say that I have written everything under compulsion.

I was a child "able to play for hours on his own," and with me "you wouldn't know there was a child in the house."

I received building blocks (bricks) when I was six. I stopped playing with them when I was fourteen.

"Aren't you ashamed of yourself? Such a big guy. You ought to be doing something else. Reading. But blocks—what next. . . ."

When I was fifteen I acquired the craze, the frenzy of reading. The world vanished, only the book existed. . . .

I talked to people a lot: to peers and to much older grownups. In Saski Park I had some really aged friends. They "admired" me. A philosopher, they said.

I conversed only with myself.

For to talk and to converse are not the same. To change one's clothes and to undress are two different things.

I undress when alone, and I converse when alone.

A quarter of an hour ago I finished my monologue in the presence of Heniek Azrylewicz. Probably for the first time in my life I told myself positively:

"I have an analytical, not an inventive, mind."

To analyze in order to know?

No.

To analyze in order to find, to get to the bottom of things?

Not that either.

Rather to analyze in order to ask further and further questions.

I ask questions of men (of infants, of the aged), I question facts, events, fates. I am not so pressed for answers, I go on to other questions—not necessarily on the same subject.

My mother used to say:

"That boy has no ambition. It's all the same to him what he wears, whether he plays with children of his own kind or with the janitor's. He is not ashamed to play with toddlers."

I used to ask my building blocks, children, grownups, what they were. I did not break toys, it did not interest me why the doll's eyes closed when it was put down. It was not the mechanism but the essence of a thing, the thing for itself, in itself.

Writing a diary or a life story I am obliged to talk, not to converse.

Now back to euthanasia.

The family of a suicide.

Euthanasia to order.

An insane man, legally incapacitated, incapable of independent decision.

A code comprising a thousand articles is needed. Life itself will dictate them. What is important is the principle: it is permissible, desirable.

On a beautiful remote island, serene, as in a fairy tale, in a fine hotel, boarding house, a suicide casts the die. Is living worthwhile?

How many days or weeks are necessary to decide? A life following the patterns of contemporary magnates? Perhaps work?

The hotel service. Duties in shifts. The work in the garden. The length of stay?

"Where is he?"

"He has left."

To a neighboring island or to the bottom of the sea.

Should there be a rule:

"The death sentence will be carried out in one month, even against your will. For you have signed an agreement, a contract with an organization, a deal with temporal life. So much the worse for you if you recant too late."

Or the death—liberation comes in sleep, in a glass of wine, while dancing, to the accompaniment of music, sudden and unexpected.

"I want to die because I'm in love."

"I long for death because I hate."

"Take my life because I am capable of neither love nor hate."

All this exists, but in crazy confusion, festering, filthy.

Death for profit, for a fixed payment, for convenience, to oblige.

Most intimately connected with death are sterilization, and the prevention and interruption of pregnancy.

"In Warsaw, you are free to have one child; in a small

171

town, two; in a village, three; in a frontier village, four. In Siberia, ten. Take your choice."

"Free to live but childless."

"Free to live but unmarried."

"Manage by yourself, pay the taxes exclusively for yourself."

"Here is a mate for you. Pick one out of ten, out of a hundred girls."

"You may have two males. We allow three females."

Hurrah! lots of jobs, files, agencies, offices!

(An iron machine does the work, provides accommodations, furniture, food, clothing. You are concerned only with organizing.)

A new method of land cultivation or livestock breeding, or new synthetic products, or the colonization of regions today inaccessible—the equator and the North and South Pole. The total population of the earth can be increased to five billion.

Communication has been established with a new planet. There is colonization. Mars, perhaps the moon will accept new immigrants. Perhaps there will be even more efficient means of communication with a distant neighbor. The result: ten billion men like you and me.

The earth has the last word as to who, where to, how many.

Today's war is a naive, though insincere, shoot-off. What is important is the great migration of peoples.

Russia's program is to mix and crossbreed. Germany's is to gather together those having a similar color of skin, hair, shape of nose, dimensions of the skull or pelvis.

Today, specialists feel the stranglehold of unemployment. There is a tragic quest for a *dish* of work for physicians and dentists.

Not enough tonsils waiting to be cut, appendixes to be taken out, teeth for filling.

"What to do? What to do?"

There is: *acetonemia, pylorospasmus*. There is: *angina pectoris*.

What will happen if we find that tuberculosis is not only curable but cured with a single injection, intravenal, intramuscular or subcutaneous?

Syphilis—test 606. Consumption, 2500. What will be left for doctors and nurses to do?

What will happen if alcohol is replaced by a whiff of gas? Machine No. 3. Price, ten zlotys. A fifty-year guarantee. The dose as prescribed on the label. Payable in installments.

If sufficient daily nourishment were contained in two x-bion pills, what about the chefs and the restaurants?

Esperanto? One daily newspaper for all peoples and all tongues. What will the linguists do, and above all, the translators and the teachers of foreign languages?

The radio—perfected. Even the most sensitive ear will detect no difference between live music and a "canned, conserved" melody.

What's going to happen when even today we need disasters to provide work and goals for just one generation?

We cannot go on like this, my dear friends. Because unprecedented stagnation will set in, and foul air such as no one has ever encountered, and frustration such as no one has ever experienced.

A theme for a short story.

Tomorrow begins a radio contest for the master violinist of the year, playing this or that symphony or dissonance.

The whole world is at the loudspeakers.

An unprecedented Olympic contest.

The fans of the violinist from the Isle of Parrots experience moments of terrible suspense.

Comes the final night.

Their favorite man is beaten.

They commit suicide, unable to reconcile themselves to the fall of their idol.

There is a Chekhov story: A ten-year-old nanny is so desperate for sleep that she strangles the screaming baby.

Poor nanny—she did not know what else to do. I have found a way. I don't hear the irritating coughing, I heartlessly ignore the aggressive and provoking behavior of the old tailor.

I don't hear it. Two o'clock in the morning. Silence. I settle down to sleep—for five hours. The rest I shall make up in the daytime.

I would like to tidy up what I have written. A tough assignment.

July 21, 1942

Tomorrow I shall be sixty-three or sixty-four years old. For some years, my father failed to obtain my birth certificate. I suffered a few difficult moments over that. Mother called it gross negligence: being a lawyer, father should not have delayed in the matter of the birth certificate.

I was named after my grandfather, his name was Hersh (Hirsh). Father had every right to call me Henryk: he himself was given the name Jozef. And to the rest of his children grandfather had given Christian names, too: Maria, Magdalena, Ludwik, Jakub, Karol. Yet he hesitated and procrastinated.

I ought to say a good deal about my father: I pursue in life that which he strove for and for which my grandfather tortured himself for many years.

174

And my mother. Later about that. I am both mother and father. That helps me to know and understand a great deal.

My great-grandfather was a glazier. I am glad: glass gives warmth and light.

It is a difficult thing to be born and to learn to live. Ahead of me is a much easier task: to die. After death, it may be difficult again, but I am not bothering about that. The last year, month or hour.

I should like to die consciously, in possession of my faculties. I don't know what I should say to the children by way of farewell. I should want to make clear to them only this—that the road is theirs to choose, freely.

Ten o'clock. Shots: two, several, two, one, several. Perhaps it is my own badly blacked out window.

But I do not stop writing.

On the contrary: it sharpens (a single shot) the thought.

July 22, 1942

Everything else has its limits, only brazen shamelessness is limitless.

The authorities have ordered the hospital in Stawki Street to be cleared. And the head doctor, a woman, was told to admit all the bad cases to Zelazna Street.

What do we do? Prompt decision, efficient action.

X and Z have 175 convalescent children. They have decided to place a third of them with me. There are more than fifteen other institutions, but ours is nearby.

And the fact that over a period of six months the lady in question stooped to every conceivable outrage against the patients for the sake of convenience, through obstinacy or stupidity, that she fought with devilish cunning against my humane and simple plan—that goes for nothing [. . .]

While I was out, Mrs. K. agreed to, and Mrs. S. proceeded to put in operation the shameless demand, detrimental in the highest degree, harmful to their children and ours [. . .].

To spit on the floor and clear out. I have long been contemplating it. More—a noose, or lead on the feet.

(It has come out incomprehensibly again. But I am too tired to write more.)

Azrylewicz died this morning. Oh, how hard it is to live, how easy to die!

July 27, 1942. Yesterday's rainbow.

Yesterday's rainbow.

A marvelous big moon over the camp of the homeless pilgrims.

Why can't I calm this unfortunate, insane quarter.

Only one brief communiqué.

The authorities might have allowed it.

Or, at worst, refused it.

Such a lucid plan.

Declare yourself, make your choice. We do not offer a choice of easy roads. No playing bridge for the time being, no sunbathing, no delicious dinners paid for with the blood of the smugglers.

Choose: either get out, or work here on the spot.

If you stay, you must do whatever may be necessary for the resettlers.

The autumn is near. They will need clothes, footwear, underwear, tools.

Anyone trying to wiggle out of it will be caught, anyone wanting to buy himself out—we shall gladly take his jewelry, foreign currency, anything of value. When he has already surrendered all—and fast—then we shall ask him again:

"Here or out there? What have you decided?"

So long as there's no sunbathing on the beaches, no bridge and no pleasant nap after reading the newspaper.

You're a social worker? All right. You can even pretend it for a time and we shall pretend to believe you. In general, we believe as long as it is convenient and whatever is convenient. Excuse me: not convenient. Whatever is in the plan.

We are running a gigantic enterprise. Its name is war. We work in a planned, disciplined manner, methodically. Your petty interests, ambitions, sentiments, whims, claims, resentments, cravings do not concern us.

Of course—a mother, a husband, a child, an old woman, a family heirloom, a favorite dish—they are all very nice, pleasant, touching. But for the present, there are more important things. When there is time to spare, we shall return to such things, too.

Meanwhile, in order not to prolong the matter, things must get a bit rough and painful, and if I may put it that way, without particular precision, elegance or even scrupulousness. Just roughly cut for current expediency.

You yourself are longing to see all this over. So are we. Therefore, don't interfere.

Jews go East. No bargaining. It is no longer the question of a Jewish grandmother but of where you are needed most—your hands, your brain, your time, your life. Grandmother. This was necessary only to hook on to something, a key, a slogan.

You say you cannot go East—you will die there. So choose something else. You are on your own, you must take the risk. For clearly we, to keep up appearances, are obliged to bar the way, to threaten, prosecute and reluctantly to punish.

And you butt in, uninvited, with a fresh wad of bank notes. We have neither time nor desire for that sort of thing. We are not playing at war, we were told to wage it with the greatest possible expedition, efficiently, as honestly as possible.

The job is not clean, or pleasant, or sweet smelling. So for the present we must be indulgent to the workers we need.

One likes vodka, another women, a third likes to boss everyone around while yet another, by contrast, is meek and lacks self-confidence.

We know: they have their vices, shortcomings. But they reported in time while you were philosophizing, procrastinating. Sorry, but the train must run on schedule, according to a timetable prepared in advance.

Here are the railroad tracks.

The Italians, the French, the Roumanians, the Czechs, the Hungarians—this way. The Japanese, the Chinese, even the Solomon Islanders, even the cannibals—the other way. Farmers, highlanders, the middle class and the intelligentsia.

We are Germans. It is not a question of the trademark but of the cost, the destination of the products.

We are the steel roller, the plow, the sickle. So long as it bears fruit. And it will, provided you don't interfere, don't whine, get all upset, poison the air. We may feel sorry for you at times, but we must use the whip, the big stick or the pencil, because there must be order.

A poster.

"Whoever does this or that—will be shot."

"Whoever does not do this or that—we will shoot."

Someone seems to be asking for it. A suicide? Too bad.

Someone else is not afraid. Hail! A hero?

Let his name shine in letters of gold but—now, out of the way since there is no alternative.

A third is afraid—livid with fear, constantly runs to the toilet, dulls himself with tobacco, liquor, women, and obstinately wants his own way. What would you do with him?

The Jews have their merits. They have talent, and Moses, and Christ, and are hard working, and Heine, are an ancient race, and progress, and Spinoza, and yeast and pioneering and generous. All true. But besides the Jews, there are other people, and there are other issues.

The Jews are important, but later—you will understand some day. Yes, we know and remember. An important issue, but not the only one.

We do not blame. It was the same with the Poles and it is the same even now with Poland and Palestine, and Malta, and Martinique, and with the respectable proletarian, and the fair sex and the orphan, with militarism and capitalism. But not all at once. There must be some order of procedure, some priorities.

It's hard for you, it's not easy for us, either. The more so since there is no buffet handy where formerly one could escape from a wearisome discussion.

You must listen my friend, to History's program speech about the new chapter.

WHY DO I CLEAR THE TABLE?

I know that many are dissatisfied at my clearing the table after meals. Even the orderlies seem to dislike it. Surely they can manage. There are enough of them. If there were not, one or two always could be added. Then why the ostentation, the obstinacy, and even maybe I'm

179

nasty enough to pretend to be diligent and so democratic.

Even worse, if anyone comes to see me on important business, I tell him to wait, saying:

"I am occupied now."

What an occupation: picking up soup bowls, spoons and plates.

But worse still is that I do it clumsily, get in the way while the second helping is being passed. I bump against those sitting tightly packed at the tables. Because of me he cannot lick clean his soup plate or the tureen. Someone may even lose his second helping. Several times something fell from the plates carried clumsily. If anyone else had done it, he would be told off and have a case against him. Because of this eccentricity some seem to feel guilty for letting me do it, others feel guilty because somehow they think they are even taking advantage of me.

How is that I myself do not understand or see how it is? How can anyone understand why I do it when right now I am writing that I know, see and understand that instead of being helpful I make a nuisance of myself?

Odd. I sense that everybody thinks I should not pick up the dishes, but nobody has ever asked why I do it. Nobody has approached me: Why do you do it? Why do you get in the way?

But here is my explanation:

When I collect the dishes myself, I can see the cracked plates, the bent spoons, the scratches on the bowls. I expedite the clearing of the tables and the side table used for the little shop, so that the orderlies can tidy up sooner. I can see how the careless diners throw about, partly in a quasi-aristocratic and partly in a churlish manner, the spoons, knives, the salt shakers and cups, instead of putting them in the right place. Sometimes I watch how the extras are distributed or who sits next to whom. And I get some ideas. For if I do something, I never do it thoughtlessly. This waiter's job is of great use to me, it's pleasant and interesting.

But not this is important. It is something quite different. Something that I have spoken and written about many times, that I have been fighting against for the past thirty years, since the inception of the Children's Home, fighting without a hope of victory, without visible effect, but I don't want to and cannot abandon that fight.

My aim is that in the Children's Home there should be no soft work or crude work, no clever or stupid work, no clean or dirty work. No work for nice young ladies or for the mob. In the Children's Home, there should be no purely physical and no purely mental workers.

At the institution at Dzielna Street run by the City Council, they look at me with shock and disgust when I shake hands with the charwoman, even when she happens to be scrubbing the stairs and her hands are wet. But frequently I forget to shake hands with Dr. K., and I have not been responding to the bows of Drs. M. and B.

I respect honest workers. To me their hands are clean and I hold their opinions in high esteem.

The washerwoman and the janitor at Krochmalna Street used to be invited to join our meetings, not just to please them but in order to take their advice and benefit from their assistance as specialists in matters which would otherwise be left unresolved, i.e. be placed under paragraph 3.[5]

There was a joke in a weekly newspaper of twenty years ago. Actually not a joke but a witty comment.

Josek—I don't remember which one, there were many

5. Par. 3 of the Home's Code read: "The Court doesn't know how it was in fact, and thus refuses to consider the case."

of them—could not solve a problem in arithmetic. He tried hard and long, and finally said:

"I don't know how to do it. I place it under paragraph three."

No one is better or wiser because he is working in the storeroom rather than pushing the wheelbarrow. No one is better or wiser just because he can wield power. I am not better or wiser for signing the passes, or donation receipts. This brainless work could be done more conscientiously and better by a youngster from third or even second grade.

The collector of money, a rude woman, is a nobody to me. Mr. Lejzor is a fine fellow though he digs in the filth of the sewage pipes and canals. Miss Nacia would deserve respect from me if she peeled potatoes instead of being a typist. And it is not my fault that Miss Irka, the nurse, shifts the inferior jobs onto Mira and that Mrs. Roza Sztokman, whom I also respect, once in a while may not scrub the toilet or the kitchen floor just to have a rest.

In farming, this is called crop rotation. In hygiene and medicine—a change of climate. In church—an act of humility. The Pope is called Holy Father, big men kneel down before him and kiss his slipper. And, once a year, the Pope washes the feet of twelve beggars in the church.

The Jews are conceited and that is why they are despised. I believe this will change, perhaps soon. Meanwhile, please don't get cross with me for collecting the dishes or emptying the buckets in the toilet.

Whoever says, "physical work is dirty work," is lying. Worse still the hypocrite who says, "No one should be ashamed of any work," but picks for himself only clean work, avoids what is described as dirty work and thinks that he should keep out of the way of dirty work.

August 1, 1942

Whenever the stems of potato plants grew excessively, a heavy roller would be dragged over them to crush them so that the fruit in the ground could ripen better.

*

Did Marcus Aurelius read the wisdom of Solomon? How soothing is the effect of his memoirs.

*

I sometimes hate, or perhaps only try to oppose, certain individuals, such as H., or G., more than Germans; from their point of view they work, or rather plan, reasonably and efficiently. They are bound to be angry because people get in their way. Get in their way foolishly.

And I get in their way, too. They are even indulgent. They simply catch you and order you to stand in one place, not to walk about the streets, not to get in the way.

They do me a favor, since roaming about I might be hit by a stray bullet. And this way I am safe standing against the wall, and can calmly and carefully observe and think—spin the web of thoughts.

So I spin the web of thoughts.

*

A blind old Jew remained at the little town of Myszyniec. Leaning on a stick, he walked among the carts, the horses, the Cossacks and the artillery guns. What a cruel thing to leave a blind old man behind.[6]

6. Again recollection of World War I.

183

"They wanted to take him along"—Nastka says. "But he put his foot down and said that he would not go because somebody must stay behind to look after the synagogue."

I struck up an acquaintance with Nastka while trying to help her find a bucket taken by a soldier who had promised to bring it back but didn't.

I am both the blind Jew and Nastka.

*

It's so soft and warm in my bed. It'll be very hard to get up. But today is Saturday, and on Saturdays I weigh the children in the morning before breakfast. Probably for the first time I am not interested in the results for the week. They ought to have put on a bit of weight. (I don't know why raw carrot was given for supper yesterday.)

*

In place of old Azrylewicz, I now have young Julek. There's liquid in his side. He has certain difficulties with breathing, but for a different reason.

Here's the very same manner of groaning, gestures, resentment against me, the same selfish and theatrical desire to attract attention, perhaps even to take revenge on me for not thinking about him.

Today Julek had the first quiet night for a week. So did I.

*

So did I. Now that every day brings so many strange and sinister experiences and sensations I have completely ceased to dream.

184

The law of equilibrium.

The day torments, the night soothes. A gratifying day, a tormented night.

I could write a monograph on the featherbed.

The peasant and the featherbed.

The proletarian and the featherbed.

*

It's been a long time since I have blessed the world. I tried to tonight. It didn't work.

I don't even know what went wrong. The purifying respirations worked more or less. But the fingers remained feeble, no energy flowing through them.

Do I believe in the effects? I do believe but not in my India! Holy India!

*

The look of this district is changing from day to day.
1. A prison
2. A plague-stricken area
3. A mating ground
4. A lunatic asylum
5. A casino. Monaco. The stake—your head.

*

What matters is that all this did happen.

The destitute beggars suspended between prison and hospital. The slave work: not only the effort of the muscles but the honor and virtue of the girl.

Debased faith, family, motherhood.

The marketing of all spiritual commodities. A stock exchange quoting the weight of conscience. An unsteady market—like onions and life today.

The children are living in constant uncertainty, in fear. "A Jew will take you away." "I'll give you away to a wicked old man." "You'll be put in a bag."

Bereavement.

Old age. Its degradation and moral decrepitude.

(Once upon a time one earned one's old age, it was good to work for it. The same with health. Now the vital forces and the years of life may be purchased. A scoundrel has a good chance of achieving gray hair.)

*

Miss Esterka.

Miss Esterka is not anxious to live either gaily or easily. She wants to live nicely. She dreams of a beautiful life.

She gave us *The Post Office* as a farewell for the time being.[7]

If she does not come back here now, we shall meet later somewhere else. I'm absolutely sure that she will serve others in the meantime in the same way as she used to distribute goodness and make herself useful here.

7. This is about the tutoress Ester Winogron, a student of natural science at Warsaw University. She helped Korczak in his daily morning medical rounds and dressings. When she was caught by the Germans on the street in the first days of the liquidation of the ghetto, Korczak tried unsuccessfully to get her out of the transport.

As for the play itself, *The Post Office* by Rabindranath Tagore, prohibited by Hitler's censors, was performed on orders from Korczak himself. The direction of Ester Winogron and the performance of the children of the Orphan's Home, especially of Abrasza in the role of the dying Hindu boy, as well as the impact of the play itself, as played in the atmosphere of the dying ghetto, in the climate of its final days—all this produced a staggering impression and an experience not to be repeated.

When after the play someone asked Korczak why he had selected this particular play, he said that, finally, it is necessary to learn to accept serenely the angel of death.

August 4, 1942

1

I have watered the flowers, the poor orphanage plants, the plants of the Jewish orphanage. The parched soil breathed with relief.

A guard watched me as I worked. Does that peaceful work of mine at six o'clock in the morning annoy him or move him?

He stands looking on, his legs wide apart.

2

All the efforts to get Esterka released have come to nothing. I was not quite sure whether in the event of success I should be doing her a favor or harm her.

"Where did she get caught?" somebody asks.

Perhaps it is not she but we who have gotten caught (having stayed).

3

I have written to the police to send Adzio away: he's mentally underdeveloped and maliciously undisciplined. We cannot afford to expose the house to the danger of his outbursts. (Collective responsibility.)

4

For Dzielna Street—a ton of coal, for the present to Rozia Abramowicz. Someone asks whether the coal will be safe there.

In reply—a smile.

5

A cloudy morning. Five thirty.

Seemingly an ordinary beginning of a day. I say to Hanna:

"Good morning!"

187

In response, a look of surprise.
I plead:
"Smile."
They are ill, pale, lung-sick smiles.

6

You drank, and plenty, gentlemen officers, you relished your drinking—here's to the blood you've shed—and dancing you jingled your medals to cheer the infamy which you were too blind to see, or rather pretended not to see.

7

My share in the Japanese war. Defeat—disaster.
In the European war—defeat—disaster.
In the World War. . . .
I don't know how and what a soldier of a victorious army feels. . . .

8

The publications to which I contributed were usually closed down, suspended, went bankrupt.

My publisher, ruined, committed suicide.

And all this not because I'm a Jew but because I was born in the East.

It might be a sad consolation that the haughty West also is not well off.

It might be but is not. I never wish anyone ill. I cannot. I don't know how it's done.

9

Our Father who art in heaven. . . .
This prayer was carved out of hunger and misery.
Our daily bread.
Bread.

Why, what I'm experiencing did happen. It happened.

They sold their belongings—for a liter of lamp oil, a kilogram of groats, a glass of vodka.

When a young Pole kindly asked me at the police station how I managed to run the blockade, I asked him whether he could not possibly do "something" for Esterka.

"You know very well I can't."

I said hastily:

"Thanks for the kind word."

This expression of gratitude is the bloodless child of poverty and degradation.

10

I am watering the flowers. My bald head in the window. What a splendid target.

He has a rifle. Why is he standing and looking on calmly?

He has no orders to shoot.

And perhaps he was a village teacher in civilian life, or a notary, a street sweeper in Leipzig, a waiter in Cologne?

What would he do if I nodded to him? Waved my hand in a friendly gesture?

Perhaps he doesn't even know that things are—as they are?

He may have arrived only yesterday, from far away. . . .

Translated from the Polish
by JERZY BACHRACH
and BARBARA KRZYWICKA (VEDDER)

STEFANIA WILCZYNSKA,
Korczak's closest associate

STAFF MEMBERS OF "CHILDREN'S HOME" WHO PERISHED TOGETHER WITH KORCZAK AND THE CHILDREN

1. Stefania Wilczynska, manager of the Children's Home since 1911.
2. Henryk Asterblum, secretary of the Board, accountant since the Home's founding.
3. Balbina (wife of Feliks) Grzyb, teacher.
4. Roza Lipiec-Jakubowska, former pupil, then for many years staff member.
5. Sabina Lejzerowicz, for many years head of the seamstress shop, then teacher.
6. Natalia Poz, pupil of the Orphanage since the age of five, then secretary and office worker of the Home.
7. Roza Sztokman, former pupil, for many years intendant, perished together with her five-year-old daughter Romcia and brother.
8. Dora Solnicka, collector of the "Help Orphans" Society.
9. Henryk Azrylewicz, Roza Sztokman's brother, office employee.

Also employed in the Home's Finance Committee was a certain Szyldwacher. He escaped during the children's deportation to Treblinka in 1942. Deported himself to Auschwitz in 1943 and appointed kapo, he refused—under threat of death—to beat his campmates, and was shot on the spot.

191

Korczak with members of his staff

*Postage stamps issued in Poland
and Israel commemorating Janusz Korczak*